A Brave Book on Kashmir

K FILE

The Conspiracy of Silence

BASHIR ASSAD

Vitasta

Thank you for choosing a Vitasta book. For years we've been committed to publishing books that inform, inspire, and endure. Reach out to us for bulk purchases. Discover more titles at www vitastapublishing.com

Published by
Renu Kaul Verma
Vitasta Publishing Pvt Ltd
4348/4C, Ansari Road, Daryaganj
New Delhi - 110 002
info@vitastapublishing.com

ISBN 978-93-86473-69-1

First Edition 2019
Fifth Edition 2026

MRP ₹495

Editor: Papri Sri Raman
Cover and layout: Somesh Kumar Mishra
Printed: Thomson Press India Ltd.

Contents

Pity The Nation
(After Khalil Gibran)

Pity the nation whose people are sheep
And whose shepherds mislead them
Pity the nation whose leaders are liars
Whose sages are silenced
And whose bigots haunt the airwaves
Pity the nation that raises not its voice
Except to praise conquerers
And acclaim the bully as hero
And aims to rule the world
By force and by torture
Pity the nation that knows
No other language but its own
And no other culture but its own
Pity the nation whose breath is money
And sleeps the sleep of the too well fed
Pity the nation oh pity the people
who allow their rights to erode
and their freedoms to be washed away
My country, tears of thee
Sweet land of liberty!

—American poet **Lawrence Ferlinghetti**
San Francisco, January 2006

For my Mother Saba

who, for fear of terrorists,
I could not visit and take care of when she was dying.
She would look fixedly at the telephone, anxiously
waiting to hear me one last time.

Publisher's Note

Article 370 of the Indian Constitution gave special status to Jammu and Kashmir, conferring it with the power to have a separate constitution, a state flag and autonomy over the internal administration of the State. Jammu and Kashmir are two regions, located in the northern part of Indian subcontinent which was administered by India as a state from 1954 to 31 October 2019, and a part of the larger region of Kashmir, which has been the subject of dispute between India, Pakistan, and China since 1947.

Article 370 was drafted in Part XXI of the Constitution: Temporary, Transitional and Special Provisions.

This article, along with Article 35A, defined that the Jammu and Kashmir State's residents live under a separate set of laws, including those related to citizenship, ownership of property, and fundamental rights, as compared to residents of other Indian States.[8] As a result of this provision, Indian citizens from other states could not purchase land or property in Jammu & Kashmir.

On 5 August 2019, the Government of India issued a constitutional order superseding the 1954 order, and making all the provisions of the Indian Constitution applicable to Jammu and Kashmir based on the resolution passed in both Houses of India's Parliament with 2/3 majority. [10][11][12][13] Following the resolutions passed in both Houses of the Parliament, the government of India issued a further order on 6 August declaring all the clauses of Article 370 except Clause 1 to be inoperative. The abrogation of a temporary rule came after 65 years.

Introduction

Manufacturing of Terrorists in Kashmir

Terrorists are not born. They are manufactured. The gruesome attack on 14 February on the CRPF convoy on the Srinagar-Jammu national highway in 2019 left the security agencies and Kashmir watchers red-faced. The attack took place at Lethpora near Pulwama, I was not surprised by this horrendous attack – the bloodiest in recent times. It was the biggest attack in the history of militancy in Kashmir. But this was anticipated, given the amount of churning and subsequent transformation of Kashmiri society over the last few decades.

How the average Kashmiris reacted to this attack is also a major marker of our times. Youth celebrated the attack silently or ceremoniously in every nook and corner of the Valley. Social media in Kashmir was flooded with celebratory messages. 'After a long time, Kashmir celebrates Valentine's Day' appeared on the Facebook wall of a sizeable section of Kashmiri youth. 'It looks like Eid', declared others. Youths took to the streets in groups in Srinagar and other cities and towns across Kashmir and burst firecrackers to celebrate the death of 45 CRPF men.

The Indian army tried to question the family members

of the suicide bomber in Pulwama village. Thousands of Kashmiris who had assembled there to celebrate didn't allow the questioning. Only a few came to denounce the attack on social media, but their number is insignificant.

Many a times, when Kashmiri mothers and sisters are asked whether they would appeal to their militant son or brother to give up arms and return to the family fold, their response is that if he returns, they will kill him with their own hands. This tells us how grave the situation in Kashmir is. Apologists will try to counter my argument by saying that there is anger against the state, and hence political radicalisation.

On 24 May 2019, the most wanted terrorist and Chief of Al Qaeda affiliate Ansar Ghazwat-ul-Hind, Zakir Musa was killed in an encounter in Tral area. One more militant was killed in the encounter. Hundreds of youth from various parts of south Kashmir on hearing the news, rushed to participate in the funeral of Musa.

Though security forces had blocked all the roads and links leading to Tral, around 10,000 people managed to reach the slain militant commander's village. Addressing the mourners, father of the slain militant, Abdul Rashid, an engineer by profession, appealed to the masses not to differentiate between militants and their organisations operating in Kashmir. 'Our mujahideen are fighting for the cause of Islam, we should not differentiate between them on the basis of their affiliations, we should stand behind them united', Rashid told the gathering. His speech went viral on social media for days together. Rashid didn't wail on seeing the dead body of his son.

On 18 June, Sajad Maqbool of Jaish-e-Muhammad, who had provided logistics for the 14 February attack, was killed in a gunfight in his native village in south Kashmir. His mother, on receiving the bullet-ridden body of his son, didn't cry in grief and pain of losing her 17-year old son. Instead, she shouted and led the procession, showing no sign of grief whatsoever. Not only this, she shouted Islamic and anti-India slogans more passionately than any professional slogan monger. It merits a mention that Sajad was a madrasa student of a well-known Deobandi School in Shopian district. This is the kind of indoctrination Kashmir has witnessed over the years. Islamists have completely transformed Kashmir, particularly south Kashmir, where parents and close relatives of militants celebrate the martyrdom achieved by their militant sons.

Can they brush aside the frequent videos released by the militants which establish that the current phase of violent uprising has more to do with global jihad than the local grievances whatsoever? Take for instance the video message of the militant Adil Ahmad, who blew himself up with 350 kg of explosives, killing around 45 CRPF personnel.

Just a few minutes *after the blast, his video was uploaded on social media. He is seen speaking with confidence about his designs and goals.* The militant is not talking about independent Kashmir or accession to Pakistan. He is talking about *jihad* and *the enemy.* Let us not be ostrich-like about the happenings in Kashmir. *There is marked influence of global jihadist Islam which the Jamaat-e-Islami and the Wahabis imported from Pakistan and Saudi Arabia respectively.*

Regarding the suicide bomb attack, the prime cause of concern is not the explosive or its preparation. It is the fact that *the suicide bomber is a Kashmiri. Multiple denominators at play here reveal that the current violent phase in Kashmir is part of the global jihad.* A few militants owing allegiance to ISIS cannot define the nature of the current violent phase, however, what defines this phase is the response of the average Kashmiri youth to the Lethpora attack.

Firstly, an attack of this magnitude could not happen without local logistic support. Most Kashmiris, particularly the youth, identify themselves with this kind of hatred for others. That the militant is a young Kashmiri is a matter of alarm. In his video, he appears completely confident and believing in what he is setting out to do. This is a matter of serious concern. It points to the severe indoctrination of Kashmiri youth. From here onwards, we should anticipate more such dangerous attacks on security forces and major installations.

When death is celebrated by a society, it needs deep analysis.

The attack led to a kind of jubilation in Kashmir. The magnitude of the damage caused by the explosive rejuvenated the Kashmiris. Till the afternoon of 14 February, they were dejected over the encounters taking place and militants getting killed, while security forces suffered no damage. After the Lethpora attack, the dominant feeling was that such intense damage to the 'enemy' could force it to flee from Kashmir.

The average Kashmiri takes every word of propaganda by militants as gospel truth.

This delusion will have dangerous consequences. On ground zero, I can see that commitment to 'the cause' has renewed after this dastardly act. The Kashmiri psyche, which outsiders often fail to understand, is weird. Hate against the Indian state has virtually transformed into a 'Hate Hindu' sentiment, compounded by strong ideological support for the deadly extremist narrative.

Fourteen February was a Friday. After the act, the enthusiasm in the mosques had to be seen to be believed. The commitment to the 'cause' resonated with the average Kashmiri. All of them may not have approved the killing of the security forces, but they would not denounce it. If some did not celebrate it, they did not mourn it too. Most Kashmiris felt that the attack was justified.

A large majority of ordinary Muslims in Kashmir feel that it is legitimate to attack the Indian security forces. We need to be very careful in understanding the Muslim Kashmiri psyche, its collective conscience. Kashmir never mourns the death of the security personnel. They see it as a predictable response to oppression committed by the Indian security forces in Kashmir.

Kashmiris are influenced by one or the other fanatical sect of Islam. Because of being influenced by the extremist form of Islam, hostile attitude towards the 'other' has a huge impact on the youth who engage in violent actions. The brute majority in Kashmir is satisfied by making the Other bleed. The entire Kashmir Muslim society agrees to use tactical violence against its perceived 'oppressor', the Indian security forces. Not all of them take to arms.

This is where the state apparatus fails to understand the dynamics of the Kashmir situation. The change has been driven by those 'peaceful' Kashmiris who provide ideological, theoretical and intellectual support to the violence. These people have either embraced Jamaat-e-Islami or Wahabism in Kashmir. Their ideological makeup makes them believe that the state run by non-Muslims can never be trusted.

'Alienation' is an essential component of the transformation of Kashmir society to the extent that it is now feeling isolated. This has gradually helped the Islamists in Kashmir to express themselves in terms of a uniform identity, viz 'Kashmiri Muslims versus Indian Hindus (kafirs)'. It is as if there never was a Kashmir that was home to Hindus or there are no Hindus in Kashmir. Pakistan has to do very little to keep the violence going. *Kashmir is becoming more and more uniform.* Efforts are on to bring in every Kashmiri within the fold of this *uniform identity* where they feel morally, politically and socially 'pure'.

The thought processes in Kashmir are synergised and unidirectional – hate India.

Scholarly institutions of traditional Islamic jurisprudence have been demolished in Kashmir. The modern Islam is essentially a political ideology. It seeks to restrict the many permutations of real Islam to a single political doctrine of exclusivity and supremacy. That is why the most outspoken Muslims are its opponents. However, in Kashmir's context, it ensures its supremacy through the use of violence. Security apparatus are not the only targets of this deadly extremist ideology. It predominantly seeks to silence the voices of dissent.

The traditional and qualified jurisprudent institutions, the certified scholars are discredited and tagged as instruments of state. The traditional Sufi Islam has been reduced to something antithetical to Islam. Shrines of sufi saints are declared unIslamic. Followers of modern theology are free to interpret Islam the way it suits them. *As for jihad, teenagers are convinced that they are engaged in a sacred war which shall take them to heaven.* The suicide bomber of Pulwama attack in his video message was confident of landing in heaven within a second of blowing himself up.

The Islamists of Jamaat and Wahabis have unleashed medieval theology in Kashmir and the younger generation, the conflict ridden, are consumed by this theology on daily basis. The efforts are to locate Kashmir somewhere in the Arabic culture being pushed forward by each sect proactive in Kashmir other than the traditional Sufism which too is losing its appeal among the younger generation – particularly in the backdrop of a vicious campaign against it. So, jurisprudence is replaced by pamphleteers. This culture has contributed largely in criminalisation of Kashmiri society. The elitist mullahs like Syed Ali Shah Geelani have a ferocious sense of entitlement and nobody can question them for the havoc wrecked by them on Kashmiri society. On 2 February 2019, a girl in Shopian district was killed in ISIS style, and the video of shooting her went viral on social media. And it is to be noted, one did not even hear a squeak from the champions of human rights in Kashmir. This is the kind of society Kashmir has become.

There are not many Muslims in Kashmir who will contest the self-pronounced decree of jihad. Hence, there are cases where the youth who took on arms are not essentially driven by oppression. In this new phase of violence, *the youth who are getting involved in violent means have no personal stories of oppression to tell. The majority now is of those who feel a moral obligation to take to arms. Kashmir is a conflict theatre that needs resolution, sooner the better, but ideological orientation of the new breed of militants should not be ignored. And the most dangerous connotation is the social sanction accorded to this ideology by extremist Islamist organisations which are mainstream now in Kashmir.*

This is the second dangerous denominator of the current phase of violence where the state has not been able to grasp what is going on. I anticipate that hundreds of youth will join militant ranks in the coming months and years on the premise of friendship and moral obligation. The set of grievances is always there. If it is not, they will manufacture new ones to fulfill their commitment to the cause. Finally, obligation to the 'Ummah' sets in, and fence-sitters too jump in to fulfill the moral and religious obligations. Even though the success rate of such violent movements is low, the ideology behind them sustains the movement. It exhausts, renews, and the cycle moves on.

Mob lynching and atrocities on the minorities in mainland India have the potential to sustain the violent uprising in Kashmir. This new set of grievances has strengthened the resolve of the Kashmiri extremist forces to wage a war against the state where 'Muslims don't feel safe'. Many political observers in mainland India say that this narrative is the largest driving force for Kashmiri extremist groups. They believe that the current phase of violence in Kashmir manifests from the insecurity felt by the minorities, particularly Muslims, in mainland India.

This is only partially true. Examine the pattern of the current violent phase in Kashmir.

It has become deadlier since 2014, with the perceptional rise in the attacks on minorities, particularly Muslims in the country. As the cow vigilante violence saw a spate of increase in the country since 2014, on the rebound, the Islamists in Kashmir have become more assertive. According to a Reuters report, a total of 63 cow vigilante attacks had occurred in India between 2010 and 2017, mostly since the Modi government came to power in 2014. In these attacks, 28 people were killed and 124 injured. In proportion, the aggressive Islamic ideology has only grown in this corresponding decade. But Kashmir has seen churning and transformation in the last many decades. Extremist Islamic groups have consolidated their ideological positions in every nook and corner of the Valley for the last half a century. Fundamentalism is the new norm. The ideological foundations of the extremist form of Islam are in full display here.

The propagation of traditional Sufi culture of Kashmir is now being seen as a conspiracy to keep Kashmiris away from the puritanical form of Islam. Educationists in Kashmir with separatist leanings have started claiming that Kashmiris never followed Sufi Islam which spoke of amity and cultural coexistence. They argue that Kashmir always followed scriptural Islam. Yet, it is from Kashmir that arose the voice that said:

I am emancipated, emancipated I am,
I am no prisoner of being born a Syed,
All the fourteen heavens are my territory,
I am slave to none.
Only they shout loud while calling others to prayer
Whose hearts are not pure.

Kashmir, being a Muslim majority region, is as susceptible to the currents of global Jihad as any other Muslim region in the world. The physical presence of Wahabis and Jamaat-e-Islami on the ground, and the fiery material available on the internet has influenced the Kashmiris to alarming levels.

A secular democratic system cannot take harsh measures to eliminate extremism. Nor can military measures alone contain the extremist forces. Extremism survives on the grievances of human rights violations. Hence security measures sometimes prove counterproductive.

The withdrawal of NATO from Afghanistan has emboldened the Kashmiri extremists, and highly violent times are anticipated ahead. Such intensive attacks as the one at Lethpora briefly unite the world, which shrinks the space for the perpetrators of violence. Briefly, it also pushes to corners the sponsors who provide logistics to the violent groups. In this situation, peace negotiations are pushed through by the world powers to avoid any major confrontation in the particular region that is affected. *But Islamic extremism directed against non-Muslim states has a unique pattern. If genuine grievances are addressed on the negotiating table, a new set of grievances is manufactured, which are essentially perceptional in character. This is done to keep the pot boiling.*

There were opportunities when the Kashmir conflict could have been resolved to the extent of satisfying the egos of stakeholders. But the new phase of violence we are going through in Kashmir has no real end game. It is as mythical and mystical in its contours as the ideologies supporting violence. The nature of the conflict has changed in Kashmir due to the growing influence of religion.

The current phase of simmering violence is driven by religious protests and by mullahs who have developed huge vested interests in the conflict. The extremist form of religion has appeal for the radicalised unemployed youth, who are ready to sacrifice their life for it.

The narrative in Kashmir is now less about the political conflict. The political conflict had resulted from faulty state policies. The massive support to the present upheaval comes from the 'Islam in danger' narrative. A strong and imaginative political leadership can make the boat sail through the most turbulent waters.

Regarding Kashmir, I was told by the government-appointed interlocutor Dineshwar Sharma that 'party interests have superseded national interest'. According to Sharma, peace initiatives are frustrated by electoral politics. Further, the attitude of the state towards peace initiatives is strongly impacted by an intensive terrorist attack like the one at Lethpora.

After the 9/11 terror attack in the US, George W Bush famously said, 'No nation can negotiate with terrorists, for there is no way to make peace with those whose goal is only death'. In the aftermath of the 14 February terrorist attack, the Indian leadership resolved to give a fitting reply to the terrorists operating from Pakistan. This way, we play into the hands of the extremist forces. They want to make the state furious and adventuristic. Under this situation, there seem to be few options left with the state to deal with extremism in Kashmir.

It is understandable that one cannot talk peace at times when one is bleeding. At such times, talk of peace is hypothetical and seems cowardly. But as John F Kennedy said, 'Let us never negotiate out of fear, but let us never fear to negotiate'.

Extremism in Kashmir cannot be fought militarily alone. There is a dire need for opening up channels of communication. These channels will revive Kashmir's peaceful, loving and tolerant society. The Indian state and the people of India are the biggest stakeholders in Kashmir. They have huge potential to do good without actually doing anything. I have learnt this after years of watching and observing Kashmir.

Casteist Mullahs Driving Deadly Narratives

THE ERSTWHILE pre-Partition Jammu and Kashmir has territories which are now part of India, Pakistan and China. The Himalyan region of Kashmir is facing a peculiar situation. Here violence has now been accorded an oblique social and religious sanction. Various schools of thought are preaching violence as the means to achieve what they aspire for. The conflict has international ramifications.

The mishandling and the 'unjustified infringement' upon the rights of the Kashmiri subjects by the state of India is a historically, politically and constitutionally established reality. Violation of the historical Delhi Agreement of 1953, erosion of Article 370 of the Indian Constitution which guaranteed special status of Jammu and Kashmir within the Union of India, farce elections, rigging of elections in 1987, the examples are many. Hence the people here have had legitimate grievances –

all political in nature. Thus, the dispute with New Delhi was political and it was essentially about the erosion of autonomy of Jammu and Kashmir guaranteed in the Constitution of India. The leadership was struggling for restoration of autonomy, as the Instrument of Accession of J&K with the Union of India was ratified by the Constituent Assembly of J&K. From this perspective, the accession of J&K with India was final.

However, dishonestly as it was on part of the Kashmiri leadership, they challenged the Instrument of Accession only because Pakistan has illegally occupied a part of the erstwhile J&K – which changed the nature of the conflict from an internal to an international one.

Misplaced political narratives of the political leadership of the time – on the provocation of a unfair election in 1987 – encouraged the youth to indulge in extremism to change the borders. Failure of the political leadership to underline the fact that re-drawing of borders was not possible, jingoistic narratives came into play. As the Pakistan-sponsored terrorism was sanctified, the narratives turned more and more Islamic. With the inception of militancy, the Islamists – particularly Jamaat-e-Islami – meticulously worked to transform Kashmir's demography and society. With the hounding of Kashmiri Pandits, Kashmir initially turned communalist. Gradually, the transformation of the society to an exclusivist, Islamist and intolerant society took place.

However, the present phase of violence in Kashmir is driven by Islamists who have transformed Kashmir into a deadly narrative with mystical, mythical, paradoxical, irrational and unreasonable goals. The bigger question before us is the tragic and alarming transformation of Kashmir's society.

Till the mid-80s, Kashmiri society was pluralist, inclusive

and a tolerant one. It is now a radical society with extreme ideological underpinnings. Killing and getting killed has been normalised in Kashmir.

How is it that a populace that was peaceful and believed in the principle of coexistence and 'live and let live' for centuries has become alarmingly violent? Today's radical extremism in Kashmir is filled with strange paradoxes and contradictions.

Since 1947, Kashmir has not been stable, but it was not violent either. The people themselves were not violent, though the land sat on the crossroad of history and had its gateways open to invading cultures and religions for thousands of years. Uncertainty always loomed over Kashmir's political landscape. How did this churning happen, that violence is now considered the legitimate means to achieve the end? Not that the provocations were not there. The infringement upon the rights guaranteed under certain treaties and covenants by the Union of India was deeply felt in Kashmir. Democratic institutions were not allowed to take root. Elections till 1987 were farce and rigged, Article 356 of the Indian Constitution was extended to Jammu and Kashmir and it was misused. Corruption was introduced as a doctrine in Kashmir the day when Sheikh Muhammad Abdullah, the then Prime Minister of Jammu and Kashmir, was arrested and Bakshi Ghulam Muhammad was installed in his position. Bakshi was given free hand to introduce corruption into the governance system. Since then corruption has been institutionalised in Kashmir.

That said, there is nothing peculiar about the psychological and social dynamics in Kashmir which justify young Kashmiri Muslims choosing death over life. Moral outrage among Generation X, alienation, a feeling of social exclusion and the collective search for a better world are global phenomenon now. Some people respond to these psychological and social phenomena violently, but they do so in an individual capacity. These violent reactions, most common in the USA and some Latin American countries, are not associated with group thinking.

An element of grievance has been seen to alienate young minds in all societies. Then why should young Kashmiri Muslims justify and glorify violence as a social response?

Before discussing the radicalisation among Kashmiri youth, it is essential to take note of the deliberate and vicious campaign by Kashmir's apologists. *Narratives have been spun as if Kashmir is the only place in the world where rights have been infringed upon. As if Kashmir is the most and only militarised zone in the world. That Kashmiri youth have been abused and alienated with no parallel in the world. So on and so forth.*

These false narratives, along with other ideological inputs, have played a very important role in the radicalisation of Kashmir society.

In Kashmir, the response of Generation X to their real and perceived grievances is violence. Most people elsewhere in the world have similar grievances against the country's regime. The difference is that young minds elsewhere channelise their energies in constructive and positive thinking. They engage in activities which relieve them of their economic and mental anxieties. There have been alarming examples where some Kashmiri youth, if they faced any negativity or challenge elsewhere in India, got home and took up arms – which have been readily available for decades, courtesy Pakistan.

Why is it that the social, psychological, economic and political factors which are common to all societies push only the Kashmiri youth in search of self-destruction? They do not push youth in other societies in this same direction.

The Kashmiri Pandit youth suffered immensely following the mass exodus. Uprooted from their homeland, they had to face very difficult situations. They could have easily produced a huge militia. That did not happen. The Kashmiri Pandits focused on education and became part of the Indian mainstream, benefitting in diverse ways.

And in contrast, Burhan Wani, who was beaten by a Border Security Force man during frisking, responded by taking up arms. Why is this peculiar phenomenon seen among Muslims alone? Why do non-Muslim youth respond differently and engage themselves in life-affirming activities under similarly testing circumstances? In the final analysis, what determines completely different response systems to the same phenomenon?

This point has to be emphasised and understood in order to understand the cycle of self-destruction taking root in Kashmir. Why is Kashmir caught in this deathly churning, a collective death-wish, when disgruntled sections of youth across all societies face similar problems?

All the alienated sections of youth all across the world have no variables that make them different from each other except one: the radical form of Islam that instigates Muslim youth to opt for violent jihad. Radicalism in Kashmir has produced a mindset that can best be described as 'finding life in death'.

The thought process is somewhat as follows:

> India is an oppressor state, it has no respect for human rights and democratic values, it has occupied Kashmir illegally, unlawfully and unconstitutionally, it has acted in breach of our religious and human rights. It has not honoured its commitment to give Kashmiris the right to choose between India and Pakistan, It has sinister plans

> to change the demography of the only Muslim majority state... so on and so forth. Hence Jihad.

This narrative has been sanctified by extremist Islamic organisations, particularly the Jamaat-e-Islami. It has evolved as the most popular narrative over the years.

There have been many violent ideologies that have existed for centuries. Leftist ideology has been highly violent in its manifestations. But radical Islam has its own logic and rationale which puts it in a unique frame. The leftist ideology resorts to violence in a totalitarian atmosphere where material deprivation is the result of political repression.

In Muslim societies, the first target is the universally accepted, appreciated and recognised form of governance – democracy. Let us study the societies under regressive occupation of external political forces, autocratic or monarchic ideologies. We have seen such societies where the leader faces repression and regression, and forces the regime to negotiate freedom, or an alternate political order.

In Muslim societies, people face the maximum outrage and repression. Leaders or ideologues instigate them from the drawing rooms. In other violent ideologies, inclusivity and accommodation is the basic premise to fight the oppressor. In radicalised Islamic societies, inclusivity, tolerance and accommodation is the first casualty. People are being mercilessly killed on the basis of their political ideologies and affiliations. This is precisely what has been happening in Kashmir since the inception of the current phase of violent unrest. Thousands of political workers of National Conference, Congress and other mainstream parties have been killed. Hundreds of thousands have been forced to give up politics.

Globally, political repression is an insufficient explanation for the emergence of violent extremism. It needs imaginative and notional grievances to sustain itself through the indoctrination of 'us and them', 'believer and the kuffar'. Here begins the desire for an ethnically 'pure state', and the return to some mythical past.

Mullah Managed

For all external purposes, Kashmiris have been – and still are – supposedly fighting for their democratic and human rights. But the forces which have been driving them to the battlefield both internally and externally are authoritarian. For decades now, these forces have drawn strength from the ideological hodgepodge of fascism, with disdain for normal politics. For instance, Mullahs from the very beginning were opposed to land reforms of Sheikh Muhammad Abdullah as they were the direct beneficiaries of the feudalism. They had developed huge vested interest in the Maharaja's autocratic rule. Maharaja Hari Singh's Independent Kashmir, Mirwaiz Yusuf Shah's accession to Pakistan and Sheikh Muhammad Abdullah's Idea of India were born essentially out of personal partisan interests of the trio. However, accession with the union of India was the only pragmatic, viable choice available with the people of Jammu and Kashmir and Sheikh was thus the leader of the masses representing political pragmatism. As Pakistan's invasion into the territory of Kashmir on 22 October 1947 made the other two options obsolete, Sheikh emerged the most popular leader of entire Jammu and Kashmir and his idea of accession with union of India, the natural choice. Therefore, the mullahs manufactured grievances and conspiracy theories to mobilise public opinion against Sheikh Abdullah.

Religious theologists within Kashmir who have driven the

deadly narratives are authoritarian in character. For decades, they have facilitated the physical elimination of hundreds of political activists who did not agree with their politics or were not influenced by such politics. This ideology is totally radical. It deliberately denies basic humanity of those whom they target. If political repression is an insufficient explanation for resorting to violence, they manufacture grievances to sustain violence.

Manufacturing conspiracy theories and consistently poisoning young minds vis-à-vis the state is also an important methodology in addition to radicalisation for sustaining violence in Kashmir.

Another important component which needs attention is the profile of those who join militancy in Kashmir. Since 2014, a narrative has been constructed by some quarters, particularly media-persons at the national level, that highly educated and technically qualified youth are taking to arms in Kashmir. After the national media, particularly TV journalists like Barkha Dutt, spun this theory, it was lapped up by the Kashmir media. It is now the dominant narrative.

This is a dangerous assumption, far from the truth. Study the family profile of most youth who took to militancy in the last four to five years. Barring exceptions, *the common thread in their family profile is religious radicalisation and poverty*. In most cases, including that of slain Hizbul militant commander Burhan Wani, it is the family background that indoctrinated the child, and led him to militancy in his youth.

Most militants have a Jamaat-e-Islami background. In south Kashmir, the Deobandi school of thought is now also playing a role in pushing the youth into militancy.[1]

There is another aspect to be studied. It is not about just the 200-odd youth who left their homes to join militancy since 2014. *The larger question is that of the militant mindset.* How has this come about? Are the excesses and human rights abuses attributed to the Indian army, the alleged denial of democratic rights by India, the weakening of democratic institutions by the local political powers the sole contributory factors to this mindset?

Is there more at play here than meets the eye?

This whole gamut must be examined from the local perspective. After the exodus of Kashmiri Pandits in the early 90s, Kashmir is now largely a homogeneous society. The pluralistic character of Kashmir society is now a thing of the past. While the Kashmiri Pandits were here, the competition was for better education. The happy intermingling of Kashmiri Muslims and Pandits have had few parallels in the world. But a positive competition was always there.

After the exodus, the competition is between the various schools of thought within the Sunni sect of Islam. After the 1990s, the competition got restricted to opening more and more madrasas and mosques, establishing one's writ in the mosques – and competition even in producing militants.

In the early 1990s, every political/religious organisation had a militant arm. Now, every religious organisation has ideological leanings backed by terrorist outfit across the border.

---

1 Islamic State theologist Mufti Shabir Ahmad Deobandi has been vocal in preaching Jihad in south Kashmir. He is on record having said on many occasions that 'we are not fighting for Azadi or Pakistan, our fight is for establishing a Caliphate'. *Times of India* reported on him exclusively in 2016 and 2017.

In the 2016 uprising, the Deobandis in south Kashmir were more active in mobilisation of youngsters than Jamaat-e-Islami. The Deobandis also developed links with Jaish-e-Muhammad across the border.

We will discuss in later chapters how the established Islamic jurisprudence in the matters of rebellion was diluted by Jamaat-e-Islami, and how every member of Jamaat – whether educated or illiterate in religious matters – was free to interpret Islam the way he pleased.

Across all of Kashmir, madrasas have come up in large numbers. Equally alarming is the pace at which Salafia mosques have come up in every single locality across Kashmir. The Salafia or Wahabi sect in Kashmir has strong ideological similarities with Saudi Wahabism.

After the murder of Moulvi Showkat Ahmad Shah, head of the Salafia sect in Kashmir in 2011, Wahabis gradually started the glorification of ISIS and its leaders. Social media is flooded with videos where the Wahabi clergy – particularly a cleric named Mushtaq Veeri of south Kashmir – is all praise for ISIS leader Abu Bakr al-Baghdadi.

For years now, social media has been fearlessly used in Kashmir for the spread of mythical and imaginative medieval ideologies. *India is currently losing the propaganda war here.* Militant organisations release propaganda videos on social media depicting highly barbaric, inhumane and sadistic behavior towards fellow human beings. These videos trend on social media and thousands in Kashmir watch them. A significant section of the society reacts to these videos with revulsion, but not all. The reason why young men and women – in fact why whole families of three generations can look at these videos and – react so differently is because what they see depicted in these videos are very different from what we see depicted, their perception and ours are different. Their political understanding is different from three generations ago, even their heaven is different from ours.

Hate ideology has crept in so deep that the killing of a 17-year old boy in Shopian was filmed by militants. The video was later shared by youth on social media in thousands with a sense of celebration. It is tragic how far Kashmir has come – *the society which only a few decades ago symbolised the most tolerant culture in the region now celebrates gory murders and shares it with family and friends.*

How can some sections of Kashmir watch the video and not be horrified or repulsed by it? The answer is that the conflict– which was political in its contours till Sheikh Abdullah was spearheading the struggle for its resolution – is now a war of 'us versus them'. It derives its strength from the radical Islam spread in Kashmir essentially by Jamaat-e-Islami from the early 1970s and joined in this by other sects including Wahabis and Deobandis in the current phase.

The problem is about perceptions. Syed Ali Geelani and the ideologues of his ilk in Kashmir have successfully indoctrinated the younger generation to a point where barbarism can be celebrated, not condemned. They see such barbarism as righteous, ritualistic retribution and retaliation against the 'oppressor'.

The Maududi ideology sees in this barbarism an unapologetic affirmation of an identity – the identity of the Muslim – which they perceive being under threat. This murderous ideology has warped the understanding of its followers towards other human beings. They find senseless killings liberating, and as empowering their own sense of identity. Such a warped worldview comes from the teachings of Maulana Maududi and his organisation's Kashmir chapter. Globally, it is seen as Salafi Islam. But in Kashmir, this murderous worldview has indoctrinated young minds through the literature and teachings of the Jamaat.

This school of thought shares characteristics with other totalitarian belief systems that are able to mobilise followers to commit brutal crimes against humanity similar to the ones that show the killings of young boys in Kashmir. The reason why this hate ideology took root at such a fast pace is well comprehended in the Kashmir context.

The traditional belief system of Sufis, followed by Kashmiri Muslims and Pandits alike, was inclined towards spiritual emancipation and inclusivity. This belief system was about coexistence, tolerance and social bonding. It had no notions of political maneuvering. This belief system had no answers for the questions that confronted Kashmir's society following post 1947 political upsurge and unrest, particularly in the aftermath of the 1975 Indira-Abdullah accord.

The form of Islam that came to Kashmir with the advent of Jamaat on the political landscape provided answers – though flawed, outdated, primitive – to the political questions. The growing influence of this ideology, particularly in schools, wrecked an unprecedented upheaval. The target group for this ideology was the age group of 15-20 years. This is the age in which individuals can be molded, because exposure to the outside world is limited and hence influence rate is high.

Contrary to the education hitherto imparted by schools, *Jamaat intoxicated the young minds about establishing Caliphate or the Islamic rule,* where problems could be solved in accordance with the teachings of Al Qur'an. In the 1980s,

Jamaat was allowed by the Indian state to established itself organisationally and started its own schools which had better facilities than ordinary schools. The primary purpose was to indoctrinate young minds with the toxic jihadist ideology. This will be discussed in detail in a later chapter.

The effort of the Jamaat was not just to introduce jihadi ideology. It was more about establishing the writ of the elitist Mullahs. Jamaat, essentially a grouping of mullahs, draws its ideological force from the practising non-Mullahs – viz. the ordinary Kashmiris. Mullahs traditionally establish themselves as saviors in the eyes of the public. The instrument for their establishment on a high pedestal are ideologically-driven ordinary Kashmiris.

It is interesting to note that the *Mullah caste* (including the Geelanis, Muftis, Shah, Handanis, Naqshbandis, Andrabis, Bukharis etc) constitute only three per cent of the Muslim population in Kashmir. Nevertheless, their visibility on the local political landscape far outpaces any other caste. *This sect of Kashmiris was the direct beneficiary of the feudal system, before the land reforms by Sheikh Abdullah.*

This caste comprised the only Kashmiri Muslims who had the qualifications to compete with Kashmiri Pandits for government jobs. They were also paid monthly remunerations by the Maharaja. That is why they were stiffly opposed to Sheikh Abdullah, who was fighting a war to abolish the feudal system. Post-1947, the elitist mullah caste initially sided with every ruler – from Bakhshi Ghulam Mohammad to Sayed Mir Qasim. Socially, they carved out a unique space for themselves. Their children were the only Kashmiri Muslims to excel in the field of education. In this way, the mullahs dominated the State bureaucracy and also the political landscape.

The majority non-mullah community remained content as second-class citizens to this 'sacred breed'. While Kashmir has been a favourite subject to write on, nobody has questioned how, when and why mullahs like Geelanis, Bukharis, Andrabis, Naqshbandis, Muftis, Hamdanis and their like dominated the political landscape in Kashmir. Despite being hardcore extremists, how this mullah clan controls the levers of power and bureaucracy in Kashmir?

It is also noteworthy that almost no member of these clans has taken to arms, got killed or abandoned their career opportunities to take part in the so-called struggle for rights. Youth from clans like Lone, Bhat, Sofi, Mir, Dar, Sheikh, Wani – all those influenced by the mullah bandwagon – steadily took to arms. Militancy survives on these non-mullah castes. *The Mullahs have survived to lead the political struggle without losing their breadwinners or their bread.*

Look at the long but exhausting list of militants active or who have been eliminated. These are the surnames you will find there – Lone, Dar, Bhat, Wani, Tantray, Turay, Sheikh, Mir and the like. Syed Ali Geelani's son, who studied in Pakistan, is not attracted towards militancy. But Manan Wani, who was studying in Aligarh, picks up the gun.

Critics may try to rip my statement apart. By doing so, they will play straight into the hypocrisy and deception prevailing in Kashmir. It suits the mullahs that nobody rakes up the harsh truth of Kashmir's society, and how the web of militancy is caste-selectively here and entangles only the young from the lower castes among Kashmiri Muslims.

The elitist, casteist mullah community has occupied every institution in Kashmir, be it government, semi-government, media, non-government or political. This clan, which has a non-Kashmiri origin, is representing Kashmir everywhere. This is the privileged sect, which is driving parallel narratives in Kashmir, representing Pakistan, India and supposedly the Kashmiris too. They are the double-dealers enjoying power and perks from both sides at the cost of the gullible Kashmiris.

The only Shah (read mullah clan) who joined militancy is Muhammad Yusuf Shah alias Syed Salahuddin. He is the head of the Hizbul Mujahideen and United Jihad Council based in Pakistan. Soon after joining militancy, he crossed over to Pakistan and established himself as the supreme commander. His seniors like Abdul Majid Dar and Master Ahsan Dar were sent back to the Valley only to be eliminated.

This casteist community believes it is destined to rule Kashmiris legitimately or illegitimately. For their survival and lavish lives, the ordinary Kashmiris have to seek eternal life in mythical and imaginative worlds they call the 'hereafter' or jannat.

Why did this murderous ideology spread at such a fast pace?

It is because the majority of the Kashmir population is Muslim and in the age of internet, the propaganda machinery is readily available. The flawed policy of the Indian state and the random human rights abuses by its forces developed a sense of victimhood among the vulnerable sections of the Kashmir population. The Islamic clergy was insensitive of what they were spreading and the Kashmiri Muslims took the response by the Indian state as attempts towards oppression of Muslims. Therefore, terrorism was accorded some sort of social sanction and the killings perpetrated by the militants are now justified and killings perpetrated by the security forces are protested to the hilt.

However, it is not about who killed whom but the larger point remains – who has authorised you to kill anyone?

The justification for killing by militants – whether those of Kashmiri pundits or of the Kashmiri Muslims on the basis of their political leanings – was a huge project continuously and constantly worked at by the Jamaat cadre. This was substantiated by the separatist leadership, particularly Geelani and his party; Jamaat-e-Islami has never ever condemned the killing of innocent people at the hands of militants.

If at all there is a statement it is under compulsion and vague, never direct. Second important thing is the new phenomenon of youth confronting the Indian security forces at the encounter sites. No one can approve of this suicidal tendency because it is very likely that anyone who comes in the line of fire can even get eliminated by a stray militant bullet. Why should someone try to disturb the operation of security forces? And if he does, the result is more than obvious. But the unfortunate part of the story is that no mullah has even bothered to issue a statement asking the youth not to venture to the encounter sites.

How can somebody trying everything to disrupt security operations and give the militants a safe passage be called or declared as a 'civilian'? And once such an obstructionist is killed in the process, there is a hue and cry over the so called 'civilian deaths'. How can the inhuman and insensitive separatist leaders be absolved? For example, the separatists called for a 'Badamibagh cantonment chalo' march on 18 December 2018. The first question is who was going to march towards the Army headquarters in Srinagar? Geelani? Geelani's son? Yasin's relatives? Mirwaiz's nears and dear ones? None among them. They would have had to enact a drama to break the

Indian security 'cordon' outside their houses which they do at every such 'chalo' occasion. Even if they walk a few steps they are protected by a huge contingent of India's security forces. What would have been the consequences if the security forces would not have sealed all the routes leading to the Army Corps headquarters? What if the Indian forces did not provide separatist leaders security?

This Badamibagh call was meant for poor gullible Kashmiris whom the leaders always exploit by invoking religious 'sentiment'.This is how they keep the vicious cycle of bloodshed going. This hostile attitude they have inculcated among the youth in Kashmir towards the 'other' seems to have very little impact on the individuals who do not want to engage in violent action. The most disturbing factor is that the dreams of many parents of those who take up arms or of those who rush to encounter sites only to get killed, shatter. Some are lured by the turnouts at the funeral processions of their beloved, but this euphoria is always short lived.

When Burhan Wani was eliminated in 2016, and the response from the youth was unprecedented and unparallel, his father was giving blessings and it gave him a solace: *Tere marne se hume mashhoor kar diya*. But when the floods of excitement receded, he found himself aloof, alone and pushed to the wall. The killing of two sons has broken his backbone and he can no more stand erect. This is the story of every father and mother in Kashmir today. Who is responsible for this? The Indian state that sent the Army to Kashmir? The separatists who instigated the gullible youth to take to arms? I have no love lost for the Indian army, but *the fact is that army and security forces dominated the civilian areas only in response to the militants imported from across the border*. The fact which no Kashmiri Muslims even dares to say is that the so-called Kashmiri leadership – particularly the mullahs – were the ones who took the first wrong step. India responded wrongly and the separatists from then on never looked back and committed wrongs one after another and projected these as 'righteous'. One can only hope, their hay day will one day come to an end.

Sheikh Muhammad Abdullah was the non-mullah leader who represented each and every section of society but empowered the real sufferers – the original Kashmiris. *He was successfully projected by the mullah community as anti-Kashmir and anti-Kashmiris.* Kashmir history bears witness that Sheikh Abdullah freed ordinary Kashmiris from the clutches of the feudal masters – the Kashmiri Pandits and the Mullah community. Mullahs, therefore, systematically maligned him in public perception. With the death of the Sheikh, the mullahs found a new lease of life. They introduced poisonous ideologies and laid the death trap for common Kashmiris, while they continued to enjoy power and wealth. And now they try hard to convince Indian Hindus that Kashmiris are anti-Indian, all Muslims are anti-India.

Is there anything 'Indigenous' in Kashmir's 'Resistance'?

A NARRATIVE has been intelligently constructed by the so-called separatist leaders in Kashmir about the mainstream political spectrum including a section of the intelligentsia. That they are stooges of New Delhi and its deep state – dancing to their tunes. Senior separatists like Geelani often use words like 'puppets' for mainstream political figures, speaking 'His Master's Voice'…so like HMV records.

Through their propaganda machinery, this narrative has trickled down to the streets in every nook and corner of the Valley. In a remote village, if somebody has a differing viewpoint not adhering to the dominant separatist narrative, he is immediately dubbed an IB (Indian Intelligence Bureau) agent. I have been witness to such incidents where a local Jamaat worker, who works in a very narrow space and has no real understanding of the outer world, speaks in highly foul language of anyone who doesn't share his world view.

In October 2018, I visited the government degree college in Kulgam in south Kashmir to seek permission of the college authorities for holding an interaction with their students. Kulgam is always in news for all the bad reasons because the area has produced a large number of militants. I was introduced by the principal of the college to one of his colleagues, who according to the principal, was in charge of the extra-curricular activities in the college.

The clean-shaven gentleman, I recalled, had spoken in a conference in Anantnag and was highly critical of the Indian state. I keenly followed him on the social media for quite some time. I was not surprised to read his posts condemning the state all the time and for his tacit support to the violence. What actually surprised me was when I saw the same gentleman doing rounds of the civil secretariat, meeting and greeting people. In June 2018, Governor's rule was imposed in Jammu and Kashmir after BJP withdrew support to the Mehbooba-led government. A few days later, I visited the Secretariat to see my friends after a long time because I had virtually stopped going to the Secretariat after Mehbooba took over as CM. It was perhaps the first day for the Advisor – Vijay Kumar – in his office. I saw this teacher from the Kulgam college waiting at the entrance of the office of Vijay Kumar, presumably to greet him. This is the height of hypocrisy. They fill the minds of the poor students with toxicity when, they themselves, enjoy paisa and power.

In 2010

During the agitation of 2010, Kashmir was on the boil. The labour class was starving for bread for their families. Education of children was badly affected. I wrote in a vernacular daily about the ground situation. I urged the so-called resistance leadership to exempt education from strike calls and provide some window to the poor vendors and labourers, so that they could earn for their starving families. It was October. The J&K Assembly was in session. I was walking to reach the Assembly, as no transport was moving on the deserted Srinagar streets.

In a while, I was surprised to see a man on a motorcycle, going in my direction. I waved to him, and he stopped. I quietly sat behind him. The man crossed over the Amira Kadal. He took the airport road at Jehangir Chowk. I asked him to drop me there, as the Assembly complex was on the other side of the road.

The gentleman had balanced something in his arms, close to his chest. As I got off the motorcycle, he said to me, 'You didn't ask me what I am holding close to my chest'. Immediately, it struck me he might be a militant carrying weapons.

Before I could say anything, he took off his helmet. With tears trickling down his cheeks, he showed me the bag. It was a Samovar, the traditional copper utensil used for serving tea. Crying, he told me, 'My mother is a cancer patient. There is nothing left in my house to buy medicines for her, as I could not go to work due to Geelani's prolonged strike calendar. I am now going to Magarmalbagh to sell the Samovar and buy medicines for my mother.'

The pain in his words seared me. I decided to go home and write about the common man's agony. I also called up Geelani and urged him to revisit his *hartal/bandh* politics, as people were literally dying. His response: 'I have received no such complaint which suggest that people are dying.'

The article appeared next day in a local daily. In the

evening, two gentlemen came to our house. One of them was a Jamaat worker, namely Ghulam Muhammad Lone. When Hizbul Mujahideen dominated Kashmir in early 1990, Lone was appointed as Nasir (Financial Advisor) for Anantnag district. Later, Lone migrated to Srinagar when militant-turned-government-renegades were ruling south Kashmir's streets. In Srinagar, he, somehow, got appointed as a government teacher. However, like other Jamaatis, Lone too didn't quit Jamaat. When Mufti Mohammad Sayeed entered into a secret deal with the Jamaat, Lone became very active and started preaching Maududi Islam in the hamlet he settled in. Lone gave the Friday sermon in the local mosque and spoke highly violent language. He referred to the article that had been published on the same day. Soon, he started shouting at me.

His volume was so high that my neighbours opened their windows to lean out and watch what was going on. The Jamaat worker was relentless in his attack.

'Manmohan Singh (then Prime Minister) has urinated in your mouth. You are anti-movement! You are an agent!' He continued screaming at me. In the midst of his diatribe, he abruptly said that Geelani Sahib's son Nassem Sahib is waiting for me outside in a car. This was his message for me.

I was trying to be politically correct, because the neighbours were watching us, and the Jamaat worker was deliberately trying to discredit me locally. Finally, I lost my cool and shouted back: 'I am satisfied about what I wrote. My conscience is clear that Geelani and his stooges like you are doing politics on human sufferings in Kashmir.'

'Your Ameer-e-Jamaat issued a statement some days ago, urging the Hurriyat leadership to allow education institutions to function. Tell me, on whose behest he gave this statement?'

The man did not understand the point I was trying to make.'What do you mean?', he shouted back.

In my turn, I too gave a loud reply, 'Go and ask him. The statement was worded at Gupkar Road (The Lutyen's circle of Srinagar). He only signed it and issued it to the media from his official fax machine!'

The Jamaat worker was red-faced and continued screaming obscenities. I retaliated at an equally high volume. 'Jamaat is an old friend of Indian intelligence agencies. Now leave my house!'

It was true then. It is true now. Yet, anyone who says anything that the separatists or Jamaatis don't approve of is labeled as 'Indian agent' in an attempt to discredit such voices. The tragedy is that the so called intelligentsia, particularly from *media whose hearts bleed for Kashmiris, have never spoken of muzzling of voice, the muzzling of dissent in Kashmir.* They content themselves with condemning the Indian state, and never question the Separatists or the Jamaatis.

In 2011

In 2011, senior journalist Seema Mustafa and her group contacted me. They suggested that we should organise a public meeting in Srinagar and invite leaders from both separatist and mainstream camps on one stage to encourage a dialogue between them. I readily agreed, and preparations for the public meeting began. I approached the management of SP Higher Secondary School for providing their auditorium for the meeting. They agreed.

The meeting was scheduled to be held in May. Many people from both camps confirmed their participation. Geelani, who was under house arrest, had not declined or confirmed as yet.

Seema, Shahid Siddiqui and others reached Srinagar two days before the event was scheduled. They insisted that I should personally go to Geelani's residence and seek his confirmation. I was reluctant, but Shahid and Seema forced me to go. I went to Geelani's house. The police party deployed there didn't allow me to go inside. On my insistence, the officer in-charge spoke to SSP Srinagar. After speaking to the SSP, he allowed me to go in.

As I entered, Geelani's men took me to a room and told me to wait. In a few minutes, Geelani walked in. Geelani greeted me, then asked, 'Aajkal Bashir Sahib kis agency ke saath hein? (For which agency are you working these days).' In the meantime, somebody served me a cup of tea, and left it on the table beside me. I gently pushed the cup towards Geelani. 'Kyun, mere ghar mein chai lene se mana kiya hai? (Have you been instructed not to have tea at my house?)'

I responded by saying, 'Where is Naseem (his son)? I want him to be here.' Geelani was taken by surprise. 'Why? Why do you want him present here?'

I answered, 'Sir, there are only two agencies proactive in Kashmir – ISI and IB. You are representing ISI, and Naseem represents IB. Take your son, go upstairs, check the lists, and certify me accordingly'.

Before Geelani could react, I said, 'I had come here to invite you for tomorrow's event and seek your confirmation. Please tell me whether you will be able to come or not'.

The separatist leadership and their followers find it easy to label anyone who differs with them as an 'Indian agent'. It is their time-tested strategy to physically and socially harm the person who doesn't agree with them.

In 2019

Now, they have further refined their strategy. The dissenter is now labeled as the 'unfaithful one' or 'Kafir'. In today's radicalised atmosphere if you are not with them, you are against them. Then you deserve whatever punishment they prescribe for you.

Today, the situation in Kashmir is that a worker of any mainstream political party is an 'infidel'. Death is the only punishment deemed fit for him. What is unique about Kashmir is that those very people who are responsible for the death of hundreds and thousands of people directly, indirectly or ideologically approve it, are self-styled 'human rights champions'.

A militant-turned-politician, Yasin Malik, during his militancy days killed scores of innocent people. Many of his victims were workers of mainstream political parties. Many were killed on the mere suspicion of being police informers. Many others he killed were Kashmiri pandits. A terrorist owing allegiance to 'Students Liberation Front' killed his octogenarian relative in judicial lockup in Anantnag in the early '90s. The aged man was in judicial custody, facing trial in a murder case. The terrorist broke the wall of the judicial lockup and killed the man. Today Yasin Malik is the champion and saviour of human rights in Kashmir.

There are numerous instances where men who killed scores of people on mere suspicion are now the torchbearers of humanity in Kashmir. Then we have another breed of sacred goats at the top. They facilitated and collaborated in the killings of men of repute and integrity, as they were their immediate competitors in the hierarchy. Unfortunately, barring one Qazi Nisar Ahmad, all the competitors who were killed were non-mullahs. 'Give a dog a bad name and kill him' is the mantra for political killings in Kashmir. Those who were killed were conveniently dubbed 'Indian agents'.

Before opening the debate on the role of deep states in conflict zones, one thing must be clear. If 'Indian agents' warrant death, what about ISI agents? Many separatists and their apologists in the media will not be able to prove that they are not ISI agents.

Kashmir has a constitutional, legal and political relationship with the union of India despite the dispute. Why is it that a so-called Indian agent is killed on mere suspicion, and the ISI agent is celebrated? Most of the mullahs in Hurriyat Conference were in touch with officials in the Indian agencies from the beginning of 1989, the year militancy broke out in Kashmir. This makes them double agents. Separatists in Kashmir behave as if the ISI has heavenly sanction and God is its supreme commander.

Life has its ironies. Acting at the enemy's behest, one may be helping the legitimate state in furthering its agenda. Geelani has taken dictates from across the border throughout his political career. In turn, he has significantly served Indian interests. Courtesy Geelani and his ilk, a matter domestically acknowledged as a 'political issue' has become a religious issue, and is now seen as Islamic terrorism. This has greatly helped India both nationally and internationally.

India has successfully – and justifiably – convinced the world that it is facing Islamic terrorism sponsored by Pakistan in Kashmir. Geelani has a great contribution in the way the issue is now labeled.

In 2016

In 2016, a senior Kashmiri bureaucrat told me something interesting. Geelani had suffered a minor cardiac arrest and was admitted in Sher-e-Kashmir Institute of Medical Sciences (SKIMS). It was in the papers the next day. The bureaucrat said that he was in the office of BR Sharma, then Home Secretary to J&K government. Sharma was later elevated as Chief Secretary.

The officer told me, 'The newspaper was lying on Sharma's table. I spotted the news that Geelani had suffered a minor heart stroke. I mockingly said, "minor? Why not major?" Sharma promptly said, "Don't say that. Geelani should survive. You don't have any idea how he is helping the state" '.

Across conflict zones globally, it is always the deep state that establishes first contacts with the rebellion groups and their overground leaders. Nelson Mandela started the dialogue with the South African deep state. Gradually, the dialogue process was upgraded. In conflict zones from North Ireland to Palestine, it is the deep state that establishes first contact.

In 1989

This is because the deep state is trained and conditioned for such functioning. The deep state initiates confidence-building at the behest of the political system. If the Kashmiri separatists established contact with the Indian deep state, or vice versa, as early as in 1989, there is nothing objectionable in it. Such is the state's conduct in conflict zones. Why should someone be killed on the mere pretext that he is in touch with Indian intelligence agencies?

Kashmiri separatist Yasin Malik was issued a passport by the Indian authorities on the recommendation of the

Intelligence agencies, to go to US for a medical check-up. The money that was collected in the name of the 'Kashmir cause' was used by him to enjoy in night clubs. Another Kashmiri separatist Shabir Shah was honoured with the label of 'Nelson Mandela of Kashmir'. He constantly and continuously engaged in dialogue with the agencies. Simultaneously, he got political workers, media persons or people from intelligentsia killed on the pretext that they were in touch with Indian agencies. I was told by none other than the then RAW Chief in 2002 that Shabir Ahmad Shah, Nayeem Khan and others were taking money from Indian agencies right from 1989.

The chief of Jamaat-e-Islami engaged in dialogue with the Indian intelligence agencies and even entered into an agreement with them on certain issues. Jamaatis, meanwhile, continued to label other Kashmiris as 'Indian agents' and facilitated their killings.

In Kashmir, or for that matter in any conflict theatre, nothing is indigenous – neither ideas nor ideals, nor idols. Politics in a conflict zone is always subservient to external forces. *Ideas are imposed. Statements are dictated from outside, and from outside come weapons.* In the Kashmir context, even those talking about complete independence from India and Pakistan got money and muscles from Pakistan. So Geelani and his cohorts are as much puppets, stooges and even 'spoons', as a mainstream leader. Geelani represents Pakistani deep state and as such is the guardian of interests of Pakistan state in Kashmir. He cannot and should not claim to represent Kashmiri interests in any manner whatsoever.

Even the idea of stone pelting was borrowed from Pakistan. What happened is that in 2005, the peace process between India and Pakistan was in full motion. Ideas of how to resolve the issues were being discussed at the track-II level and the political leadership of both the countries was monitoring the progress very keenly. Owing to his commitment to the process and also because of the pressure from the US, President Musharraf wrote to the Kashmiri separatists, making his intention clear – that he wanted to end the cross-border conflict. He suggested that the separatists should recourse to Palestanian-type Intifada. The letter from Musharraf was delivered to the separatists by a Pakistani senator, MP Bhandara.

Though stone-pelting was massively resorted to in 2008 but Yasin Malik did not wait that long. In his Maisuma locality, people were taken aback when a handful of youth in the locality would resort to stone-pelting every day, whether there was any provocations from the paramilitary troops deployed in the area or not.

A significant number of Kashmir watchers internationally say, the separatists must maintain neutrality if they are concerned about the resolution of the conflict. They have consistently maintained that peace cannot be achieved in Kashmir unless Kashmiri leaders stop representing Pakistan.

What does that mean? It means that the separatist leaders will have to condemn each and every inhuman act perpetrated by the militants. They will have to highlight the atrocities committed by the militants on Kashmir in the same spirit that they highlight the excesses by the Indian security forces.

Will they do it? No, because they are His Master's Voice in Kashmir. They cannot move an inch beyond what Pakistani agencies entrust them with. They can't be peace-brokers, because Pakistan does not want that. Rather, Pakistan will not allow it to happen.

A Kashmir lover needs to ask, then what is the fun of investing in them in brokering peace?

This has been my constant argument with the Delhi intelligentsia. Whenever the Kashmir situation worsens, the secular, liberal section of the Indian media starts pitching for a *dialogue with the separatists.* They have failed to understand a fundamental truth about Kashmir. If they want Kashmir to be peaceful, they should convince the Indian government to start dialogue with Pakistan. This should be their primary concern. Meeting Geelani and others for brokering peace in Kashmir is like asking Mohan Bhagwat to give up on his Hindutva agenda. Can Bhagwat afford to do so? No, because RSS is the ideological anchor for Hindutva.

The same holds true for Kashmiri separatists.

A senior separatist leader, a non-mullah, said as much in 2016 when I took a delegation of senior journalists from Delhi to meet him. As the guests were leaving his house after the meeting, he held my hand, pulled me and said, 'what do they expect from us? Who are we? Tell them to talk to Pakistan and ignore us'.

The claim that the separatists represent Kashmiris has to be demolished. They don't represent Kashmiris politically. But yes, they do exploit the emotions of Kashmiris to suit their agenda.

Common Kashmiris above the age of 40 know that the separatists aren't their true representatives. They also know that re-drawing the borders is impossible. An element of fear and intimidation has crept into them to the extent that collectively, they shout, '*Hum kya chahte, azadi*!'

Individually, they say that 'nothing is going to happen'. Is this dilemma? No. It is fear of the gun. It is threat to life which forces them to echo the azadi slogan in public, and negate it in private conversations. You are free to publicly condemn, criticise, curse and abuse India as much as you can. The more the better. But if you publicly say a word about the futility of this bloodbath, you will soon find yourself in the hit-list of terrorists. Any hard-hitting anti-movement talk and consider yourself dead.

Two Mainstream Voices

The mainstream voices in Kashmir blame New Delhi for its flawed Kashmir policy. National Conference led by Farooq Abdullah and Peoples Democratic Party led by Mehbooba Mufti boycotted the municipal and panchayat elections in the State, held from October to December 2018. NC and PDP have often warned New Delhi of the consequence of a flawed policy.

In Kashmir, in addition to condemning India, people also enjoy much freedom to abuse, accuse and blame the mainstream leadership in Kashmir. Some sympathisers of separatists on social media seem to lose their humanity while lashing out at Mehbooba. Attacking the mainstream is a freedom Kashmiris enjoy, so they have been doing it for long. Do they have even one-tenth of this freedom to condemn Geelani? Absolutely not. Remember I am referring to the older generation, the generation which has seen many storms in the tea cup, the generation which has seen normal times and happier days before 1989.

Leave aside Geelani. Go to south Kashmir and conduct a survey. See if anyone dares to criticise a local Jamaat leader, and does he stay safe?

Freedom Struggle Snatches Freedom

The first characteristics of the 'freedom struggle' in Kashmir is to snatch whatever freedoms people enjoy in India. *Since the 1990s, hundreds of innocent people have been killed on the recommendations of the local Jamaat units.*

Look at the extent of suppression and subjugation in Kashmir. There are families, whose loved ones were killed by militants known to them. The survivors cannot complain against the militants, such is the fear. In conflict-ridden Kashmir, everything is fake and imported – barring one thing: the sentiments of the gullible Kashmiris.

Why do I repeatedly use the word *gullible*? It has a context. A survey should be conducted across Kashmir to check how many mullahs or their children have ever participated in peaceful protests or demonstrations, leave alone stone-pelting? The survey will reveal the truth – not a single mullah or his children come out to protest.

Then the next survey. How many mullahs condemn the action of security forces over the use of 'force' on the protesters? How many mullahs lead the protests from their drawing rooms? Almost everyone. Geelani, Hamdani, Bukhari, Indrabi, Naqshbandi – all of them are found shouting on prime time over the 'excessive use of force' on the protesters.

Write-ups condemning and further exploiting the emotions of gullible Kashmiris – all these come from the mullahs. A man called Javed Iqbal who spent 45 years in Iran as a doctor, made a fortune and settled his children well, returned to Kashmir at the fag end of his life to represent the 'sentiments of Kashmiris' on almost daily basis in newspapers. Another man called Sayed Shakeel Qalander was appointed a member of the C Rangarajan Committee on Kashmir (that submitted its report to government in 2007) by the Manmohan Singh government, to advise on economic matters pertaining to Kashmir. Suddenly, the man became the champion of the Kashmiris' right to self-determination. Why? Because he is a mullah.

In 2017

In 2016, the mullahs of Kashmir and their sympathetic media constructed the 'now or never' narrative. It drew people deep into the dark tunnel of human suffering. By the time the agitation ebbed, it had consumed 150 young lives, had blinded around 1,000 people and damaged public and private property worth lakhs of crores of rupees.

I called on a so-called civil society member and businessman who had been given a contract worth crores for constructing shelter-homes for Pandit migrant families working in Kashmir under special recruitment package. The gentleman was spearheading the narrative of '*abhi nahi to kabhi nahi*'. Now or never. I told him, the 'now' has not happened. On a public platform, let us debate the '*kabhi nahi*' part of your slogan. 'You have to answer and you have to be accountable for your call', I told him.

I suggested to him that I will organise a conference in Kashmir in January 2017. My purpose was that he and his cohorts, together in this project of death and destruction, should explain what they had achieved through this unmindful madness. I knew they would not come forward to be held accountable now.

In January 2018, my organisation *Lehar* organised a conference on the theme 'Kashmir Conundrum: Stakes and Stakeholders'. The said gentleman was there with the rest of his group. I had invited Siddharth Vardarajan, Shahid Siddiqui and others for the conference. Speaking at the conference, Prof Hameeda Nayeem of Kashmir University lambasted Siddharth for his statement that the Indian army was a stakeholder in the Kashmir conflict. At the end of the conference, I took Nayeema aside and told her, 'Madam you can give me a bad name and get me killed. I am not an agent of either India or Pakistan. My conscience is clear. My heart bleeds on watching the Kashmiri children getting killed after the hot and rebellious speeches given by senior people like you. The truth is you and your husband Nayeem Khan are the double-agents taking money from both India and Pakistan for sustaining the bloodbath in Kashmir.'

The mullahs, a miniscule minority in Kashmir, are grinding their own axe in the name of the so-called freedom struggle.

They have diligently safeguarded the future of their kith and kin while fueling the miseries of the common masses in the name of azadi. This is the unfortunate part of the Kashmir Story. There was hope after the despotic, autocratic rule of the Maharaja ended in 1947. There was hope that the nightmare had passed, and bright future lay ahead. But Kashmir's elitist mullahs, in connivance with forces across the border, shattered all hopes, and the State fell apart. Since then, there is no end to the miseries inflicted upon the Kashmiris. The State is under constant siege mentally and politically.

The current phase of bloody violence has proved that Kashmiris have learned no lessons.

We have chosen new ring masters and jugglers who make us dance to their tunes. We still act as robots and play into their hands. Our ring masters have developed huge interest in keeping the Kashmir pot boiling. They give strike calls and we comply meekly even as our children suffer. They flood our mosques with fiery talk, constantly shouting about injustice and revenge. We don't dare to question them nor even think of God.

We hate them, but we never utter a word out of fear.

We do not realise that our children sitting by our side in

the same mosques and madrasas are influenced by this violent, hateful talk. They find glory in fighting this so-called injustice and revenge. We have no guts to ask these Geelanis, Bukharis, Shahs, Indrabis, Hamdanis and Sayeds why jihad is forbidden for their kith and kin. Having pushed us and our children in the den of death and destruction, they send their own children abroad for higher studies, jobs and business. How have the mullahs built for themselves palatial bungalows, hotels, malls, showrooms without any visible source of steady income? Why are the sons and daughters of Geelani and his ilk destined to be doctors, forest officers, bureaucrats, academicians, entrepreneurs, while the children of the common Kashmiris die in the streets for freedom and jihad pelting stones?

The answer is simple. They find life in our death. And they made us believe that in death lies our life.

Role of Teachers in Indoctrinating Young Minds

WHILE DISCUSSING the religious radicalisation among the youth, academics agree that this happens predominantly in regions of impoverishment, violence, political volatility and uncertainty. The indoctrination is markedly intense among the youth who have limited education and face lack of work opportunities.

Regions of violent conflict create the 'desired' conditions. The youth become ready prey where they lack a safe and secure environment, and opportunities for positive development. The social stratification exacerbates these conditions and leaves these vulnerable youth in a Catch-22 situation. For a section of these youth, the only channels of advancement remain the unlawful and violent ones.

Taking terrorism in Pakistan as a case study, it has been

observed that terrorist organisations mainly originated as a result of the state supporting terrorist groups in its neighbouring countries like Afghanistan. Consequently, the country became a hotbed for Muslim Jihad and the training of jihadis.

The toxic religious atmosphere in Pakistan cannot be explained entirely through the existence of jihadist training camps on the peripheries of its borders.

Alongside its frontiers with Afghanistan and India, and within Pakistan itself, the state supports a phenomenal number of madrasas. Madrasas are Islamic seminaries which teach Islam-related subjects such as the memorisation and interpretation of the Quran, the principles of Islamic jurisprudence and the sayings of Prophet Muhammad. The national curriculum of Pakistan was Islamised during the 1980s under General Mohammad Zia-ul-Haq, a military ruler who promoted Pakistan's Islamic identity in order to bring together a mix of tribes, ethnicities and languages. The majority of madrasas in Pakistan are Sunni, following the doctrine of the orthodox Deobandi sect.

'Education in Pakistan was left to the dogs' is what was famously stated by Pervez Hoodbhoy, a physics professor at Quaid-e-Azam University in Islamabad and a prominent activist concerned with promotion of freedom of speech, secularism and education in Pakistan. Hoodbhoy has been a consistent critic of the government's failure to oppose the spreading of Islamic militancy and promote educational improvement initiatives.

Shia vs Sunni

With few avenues for advancement and conditions of despair and neglect, religious schools find a void that needs to be filled. Notably, Saudi Arabia has a history of funding many madrasas, especially those that promote Wahabism. Saudi Arabia's initial aim, when it started providing help in the mid-1980s, was to counteract the aid that the (Shiite) Islamic Republic of Iran was delivering to the Shia minority in Pakistan. Saudi Arabia stepped in with generous supplies of financial capital in order to expand the number of conservative Sunni madrasas.

The processes of radicalisation and indoctrination have multiple layers. Under the layers exists a complex picture, where numerous social factors are involved, such as group identity, individual roles, socio-economic status, political and religious beliefs, motivations and predispositions. Radicalisation appears to be an extremely fluid phenomenon – one where change of attitude and outlook is the benchmark.

We restrict our discussion on the radicalsation of young minds in Kashmir. Much has been written on the Saudi-funded radicalisation. There is an interesting and also astounding observation about radicalisation in Kashmir. The atmosphere for it was conducive. Extremist ideologies imported from the schools run by Jamaat-e-Islami spread to the government educational institutions at an alarming pace. In the Indian context, RSS is infiltrating into government institutions all across the country with the facilitation of the present BJP government. In many cases, RSS has completely taken over vital institutions. Their intrusion cannot be attributed to wrong appointments or government-sponsored intrusion alone. In many cases, such individuals occupy decisive positions through appointment on merit, or appointment through the legitimate process. The vital thing is that they are now part of the system.

In Kashmir, the intrusion of Jamaat-indoctrinated cadre in the government institutions – particularly in government schools – dates back to when Maududi[2] literature was made available in Kashmir in 1965, and in abundance after 1977. The rate of intrusion increased alarmingly with the advent of armed insurgency in 1989.

In 1992, the government banned Jamaat-e-Islami and its Falah-e-Aam Trust, its educational wing, for indulging in anti-social activities. *Simultaneously, the government issued the order for absorption of teachers of the Falah-e-Aam Trust in government schools. Here began the Jamaat onslaught in government schools.* This is not the only window through which the Jamaat cadre crept into government institutions. A large number of individuals believing in the Jamaat ideology got appointed as teachers and even as assistant professors on merit. They secured most number of jobs in the Education Department. The administration of Kashmir was already firmly in the hands of elitist mullahs, including the mullahs who believed in the ideology of Jamaat-e-Islami. In the 1990s, it became a cohort of mullahs and ulamas(teachers) whose stranglehold on Kashmiri society is today near-impossible to shake off.

Which Teacher Knows Islam Most?

In government schools in Kashmir, both at primary and higher secondary level, there is an unspoken competition among teachers as to who has more knowledge about Islam. This culture is so pervasive that even teachers with a secular mindset have been influenced by Maududi Islam.

Another unique practice has developed over the years in Kashmir. People talk about Islam all the time, regardless of

---

2 Syed Abul A'la Maududi Chishti.

whether they follow its noble tenets in their personal lives. Such people who speak constantly about Islam are the ones who are most respected and heard.

Coming back to the teachers. Yes, Kashmir has those government teachers too, who try their best to impart quality education to their students. But they are outnumbered by the Islam experts among them. Such teachers enter the classroom more to impress their pupils about their Muslim identity than to provide them with education – the job they have been appointed for. The primary concern of such a teachers is to teach *his* version of Islam rather than engage with the curriculum. The age of 12 to 20 is the most vulnerable. Children and youth are quick to get influenced, since they are not mature enough to decide what is right for them.

The children of these Islam-expert teachers, meanwhile, study in posh English-medium private schools in the Valley, where the emphasis is on quality education. A prominent Jamaat-e-Islami member, Assadullah Bhat, in my hometown, was on the advisory body of Jamaat for years. He had been a government teacher earlier. In his Friday speeches, he would spread venom about the Delhi Public School group, labeling them un-Islamic, or rather anti-Islamic. He would appeal to parents not to send their children to any branch of Delhi Public School in Kashmir. His three grandchildren studied in DPS Budgam and DPS Srinagar.

Such government teachers provide a comparatively safe school environment to their own wards, while they engage in hatemongering at their work-places. The children of majority of Jamaat leaders occupy respectable positions in government departments. This is because they enabled their own children to focus on education.

Back in the government schools and mdrasas, they poison the minds of poor children and at times, even instigate them. This is one of the significant points where the stone-pelting by students finds its ideological input. The other places where children receive such indoctrination are their home environment and peer influence. Hence, we find instances where students leave for the school in the morning, but don't return home. The next day, their photograph holding an AK 47 goes viral on social media.

During an interaction organised by Lehar with youth in colleges, I saw a peculiar reaction at work. Every time we started a dialogue with the youth, we found that they first expressed themselves through the language of anger and hostility. But with sustained interaction, after you put forward your point gently and rationally, you can see them getting serious and contemplative about new ideas.

At this point, I also saw a strange teacher-student interaction emerging at some places. I saw that when the teacher, particular one from a Jamaat background, got the feeling that his students had started introspecting and analysing new ideas, he or she would bursts into anger and vitiate the atmosphere by an emotional outburst. This was deliberate and intentional – and unmindful of the sufferings and miseries of the people in Kashmir. *With these teachers getting a high monthly salary and their wards getting quality education in private schools, a change in the mindset of poor students was not their concern.*

At some conferences and public meetings, I was happy to see teachers who would respond positively to discussion of new ideas and encourage their students to engage in positive debate of ideas.

Competing Madrasa Culture

The second important factor which greatly contributes to the radicalisation of young children is the competing madrasa culture. *These madrasas are mainly meant for the children who come from a very poor background. It is tragic to see the so-called ideologues of almost all sects of Islam targeting poor Kashmiris and convincing them that their impoverishment is a direct consequence of their deviation from the true path of Islam.* They consistently work at convincing the parents that the only way to redeem their sins is through devoting the lives of their children to Islam. The teacher proposes to educate these children at his madrasa and subsequently promises to *find them employment in the service of Islam.*

Madrasas in Pakistan's tribal areas, and those in Kashmir have a major difference. In Pakistan's tribal areas, parents are convinced about their salvation through the martyrdom of their children. In Kashmir, the argument is salvation through devotion. The madrasa management never talks about jihad or martyrdom directly with parents in Kashmir. Once the parents give consent, everything comes up in the discourse. After many years of little or no contact with the outside world, madrasa students become highly devoted to their masters.

The authoritarian doctrinaire education established through memorisation inhibits expression of free thought or individual will. It gives wide space to religious fanaticism and incites a desire to confront anyone pointed out as an unbeliever by the teacher. Madrasas are usually in remote areas. They maintain a limited number of students so that they do not draw attention. Children are indoctrinated in sectarian extremism, hatred for non-Muslims, and anti-western beliefs – barring honourable exceptions. The recruiting teacher occasionally visits the families in order to give them a glorious account of the ward's progress and reassure the parents that this was the best decision they took for their children.

Use of Modern Technology for Radical Ideas

Modern technologies further facilitate the groups' objectives and strengthen the mechanisms of radicalisation.

Information-sharing has aided in the spread of extremist beliefs at an alarming pace globally. Social media is an important instrument in the radicalisation of youth and their subsequent recruitment as terrorists. These groups seduce the youth with the assurance that under their wing, they will find understanding, recognition and a sense of purpose.

Kashmir has been deeply impacted by indoctrination. The news of someone being killed by security forces in collateral damage; pictures of militants killed in encounters; comments on social media romanticising the death of the militants; videos with large crowds participating in the last rites of a slain militant; people chanting slogans during the funeral of a militant – all has become part of normal discourse even in economically-deprived families.

In the madrasa, things acquire greater emphasis, with the madrasa teacher sharing with his students the videos and comments on social media. Again, barring honourable exceptions, this works towards invoking extremist tendencies.

Children from under-privileged and disadvantaged sections of the society join madrasas. Group thinking becomes a mighty force, and the decision-making is similarly influenced. Inflammable material is quickly posted on social media and spreads fast. Users become outraged, comment on the material, open a discussion on it and share links. Youth outraged by the action want quick retribution, and resort to violent means. *In government schools, poor academic performance, indoctrination at home or by teachers, relentless social media campaigns, lack of purpose in life are among the reasons that drive Kashmiri youth to take up militancy.*

Whither the Famed Islamic Jurisprudence

The fundamentals of Islamic jurisprudence have been negated and deeply eroded by the Maududi cult in Kashmir. The teaching community influenced by Jamaat ideology interprets Islam in a way that gives every individual the right to proclaim anyone as infidel and *takfeer*. According to this ideology, anyone who does not agree with you is an infidel and deserves to be killed.

In November 2010, a member of Jamaat-e-Islami, who was professionally a school teacher, intimidated me and declared that I was an infidel. He issued a verbal decree, saying that my *nikah* with my wife was now illegitimate, because my wife was from the Jamaat background and I had rejected that ideology. He issued the decree that I was 'wajibul qatal ' (due to be killed) because I was not in agreement with their ideology. One can imagine how this teacher would be poisoning young minds, and how he would have inculcated this murderous ideology among his students.

On 25 December 2018, I met a friend, who has retired as a school teacher. He is from Jamaat background. I had just entered his rented accommodation at Jammu when another retired teacher dropped in. He was a Jamaati too. The owner of the house was also a teacher, but not a Jamaati. The visiting fellow asked the owner of the house, 'Is it a holiday today?' The owner told him, 'Yes. It is Christmas today, the birthday of Jesus.' The visiting teacher got furious and shouted at him in Kashmiri, 'No! It is not the birthday of Jesus. There is no proof in Quran, the teachings of the Prophet or in Bible that Jesus was born on 25 December. This is absolutely wrong. We should raise our voice against this false narrative that Jesus was born on this day.'

'Who are you to decide about the faith of others', I asked the shouting man. 'How can you infringe upon something which has to do with others' faith? How can you impose your worldview on others? Who has given you this right?'

But I can question or confront only one man, or a few such men. I feel sad for students who have been taught by such teachers. I have seen the hostility that has been bred in young Kashmiris towards all 'others'.

What does Toxic World View have to do with Kashmir's Political Dispute?

What does this toxic worldview have to do with the so-called 'political dispute' of Kashmir? I once asked a senior Kashmir politician, 'Had this conflict not been there, or if it had been resolved in the 1970s, would Kashmir be peaceful today?' He couldn't answer my question with conviction. I told him that in my opinion, Kashmir would still be in flames because such a narrow religious worldview has settled in, in our collective social mindset.

Teachers influenced by the Maududi sect of Islam, or those adhering to it, have aided in the erosion of Kashmir's secular, inclusive culture. I have seen people embracing Maududism, influenced by the feeling that non-adherents will result in them facing isolation. Jamaat invests in uniform group identity. People find it difficult to distinguish themselves from dominant social groups through non-engagement. The Jamaatis, in turn, do not want to engage with those who do not adhere to their version of Islam. Nevertheless, efforts at indoctrination are consistent and continuous, on account of their ardent desire to see all Muslims accept their version of Islam.

I have repeatedly got the feedback that teachers holding the Maududi worldview resort to character assassination of their fellow-teachers in classrooms, leaving little scope for students to respect an alternate worldview. They go all out with an onslaught on 'others'. Due to fear of violence, those at the receiving end do not resist or oppose in any way. This exclusivist world view takes strong roots in the minds of the youth. A hatred for all 'others' colours their social perspective.

While securing safe environs for their own children in private schools, these teachers remain committed to the mythical 'hereafter', rather than tutoring their students to navigate the real world. *'Azab e qabar', meaning punishment in the grave is widely discussed over the morning assembly in schools, without sensitivity towards the tender age of students.*

Such systemic grim talk has led to psychological disorders among children in Kashmir. Their worldview gets confined to the mystical and mythical 'hereafter'. Driven by diverse factors, they are easily led to violence in search of 'eternal peace'. I am conscious that when this book gets published, these narrow-minded followers of Maududi will declare me an infidel by describing my book as an attack on Islam. I have no intention to hurt anybody's faith. But for these Maududis and all others who propagate hateful ideologies, charity must begin from home. If these hate-mongers believe that what they preach is good for humanity, they should make their own children practice it. Why should only the children of the poor alone be subject to this ideological anathema?

Retired Govt Servants on the Forefront of Dangerous Narratives

THE BUREAUCRACY in Jammu and Kashmir, particularly the Kashmir section, has rarely been pro-people. It is popularly believed that corruption, nepotism and favouritism have been state policy from the time when Bakhshi Ghulam Mohammad was installed as the Prime Minister of Kashmir after the coup in which Sheikh Muhammad Abdullah was arrested in 1953. The corrupt bureaucracy is infamously referred to as *afsarshahi* in Kashmir.

Since 1953

The word *afsarshahi* fully captures the Kashmir scenario – enjoying power to the hilt without accountability to the general public. Corruption in departments like revenue, police, education, public works, social welfare and other departments is both endemic and epidemic. Just like in the rest of India for the last 70 years. *Afsarshahi* from top to bottom has legalised corruption in government institutions. The quality of services provided is always poor. People are not benefitted by welfare schemes, given the scale of corruption, nepotism and favouritism in the departments which execute these schemes.

Corruption has damaged the State beyond redemption. This is a major factor which has contributed to the alienation of Kashmiri youth. During its tenure, the Mehbooba Mufti-led PDP-BJP coalition government damaged institutions further by resorting to backdoor appointments, where money transactions were stated to be in crores. The beneficiaries were Mehbooba's coterie of bureaucrats and politicians. After a whole career marred by corruption and nepotism, Kashmiri bureaucrats – even those at lower ranks – find it difficult to have acceptability among social circles or in their neighbourhoods after retirement. Now they have to live with the same people whom they would not entertain while in office.

Barring some honourable exceptions, the bureaucrats siphon off as much as they can from the State coffers. Most of them build assets in Jammu and also in other States. But they want to live their retired life in their beloved Valley. Then there is another factor. *These people, who drew fat and pensionable salaries, worked for Bharat Sarkar. They were instruments of Bharat Sarkar in Kashmir.* Combined with corruption, nepotism and favouritism which they blatantly indulged in, they also have to now distance themselves from the same Bharat Sarkar. None of them have forfeited their pension to sincerely distance themselves from the Indian government – though they try so hard to project distance from India.

To create space and acceptability, this section of Kashmir

society has invented an interesting formula. *Once they retire, they immediately take refuge in the mosque and become instrumental in spearheading the narratives of religious bigotry.* It is the story of almost every retired government servant. He creates space for himself in the mosque management committee. Here, his lifelong administrative skills help him rise to the top. With nothing at stake, the retired government servant collaborates in constructing dangerous narratives of 'us' and 'them'. Having done the needful during service to settle their children, the gentleman now is free to invoke the 'Islam in danger' narrative.

These people often narrate anecdotes – true or concocted – of how they were suppressed or oppressed by the 'other' during their service period. They play the victimhood card and control the mosque. *During the years of street violence in Kashmir – 2008, 2009, 2010, 2016 and 2018, retired government servants played to the hilt the narrative of 'no education till liberation'. Their children were adults by then and gainfully employed, so they were not impacted by these misdirected slogans.* Hence, the retired government servants become the pillars of 'Islam in danger' narrative.

This tribe has significantly contributed in replacing the azadi narrative with 'us and them' narrative. This narrative is pinned on hate-mongering and spreading negativity about others. Some retired civil servants have formed civil society groups, where the hate campaigns continue. A retired Inspector General of Police, infamously known as Farooq Military who was notoriously involved in dozens of extra judicial killings, now calls upon the faithful five times every day, giving *azaan* at a newly-developed posh area mosque where many high-profile retired bureaucrats and politicians reside.

This large chunk of retired Kashmiri government servants find refuge in misplaced narratives. They contribute in sustaining the violence in Kashmir for their petty interests, pushing the youth into the minefield. One can see them vociferous and visible in strengthening the dangerous narratives of 'us and them', and 'Islam in danger'.

During the 2016 unrest, I saw the same phenomenon playing out. A number of retired government officers were at the forefront, asserting that educational institutions must remain closed till the Government of India accepts defeat and negotiates resolution with the Hurriyat. I confronted many of them and found their personal accounts to be the same. Their children are well-settled overseas, and they have nothing at stake. Such dichotomy across Kashmir prompted me to write this book. You secure the future of your own children and now push the children of others into the battlefield.

What is at play here? These retired civil servants don't want to see the children of poor Kashmiris excelling in education and competing with the children of the privileged class, which includes these retired government servants and also the Kashmiri mullahs. *When will the poor Kashmiris people realise this? When will they exercise authority and stop their children from walking into the death trap laid by this privileged section of the society?* A senior serving bureaucrat, Ashraf Bukhari who faces corruption charges, constructed a unique conspiracy theory over the killing of a senior journalist, Shujaat Bukhari.

As I was working on this chapter, a former senior bureaucrat, Muhammad Shafi Pandith – who retired as chairman, Jammu and Kashmir Public Service Commission which is equivalent to the Chief Secretary's post – came out with a statement which was carried by many vernacular newspapers condemning the anti-encroachment drive initiated by the department of Irrigation and Flood Control, Kashmir. Since the demolition drive touched his skin, the former bureaucrat manufactured everything to question the validity of the drive. But what was astounding was the last part of his statement which reads, 'or does this illegal drive suggest that in tune with the current policy of the deep state, the officials of the irrigation and flood control department have, in order to prove that they are more loyal than king, decided to deny the basic fundamental rights to the citizens of the State?'

One can imagine to what extent a retired bureaucrat can go in defending himself. Criticising or for that matter condemning the action is acceptable to the extent of questioning it on procedural basis but turning it into a ploy of the Indian deep state is reprehensible. This is how the retired government servants exploit the situation in Kashmir to create a space for themselves. 'Give the dog a bad name and kill him.'

Once they retire, religion and politics is the most dominant theme which occupies almost all social and mental space. Now these ex-bureaucrats are the preachers of political Islam, spreading venom and hatred, and the example of the retired senior bureaucrat's statement on the demolition drive is just the tip of the iceberg. Politics and religion are now like their life and soul, it is really a big challenge to face this manufactured and fake 'obsession with Islam' on a daily basis.

A young KAS officer who was secretary in the State Services Selection Board refused to respond to an official query of a group of aggrieved candidates for a year-and-a-half. He made them suffer mentally all this time. The youth got a response from the department only after he was transferred. But this same officer always maintains that India has alienated the youth in Kashmir. Such is the hypocrisy that we see on a daily basis. *Government officers in Kashmir do not process files for months and years together. The applicant may keep making rounds of the department for years. And yet they blame the Indian state for all the ills faced by Kashmir.*

Public delivery system in Kashmir is shockingly inefficient. *The officers in authority make no effort to make life easy for their fellow Kashmiris. In cursing the Indian state, they take the moral high ground.* The damage inflicted by the Indian state in Kashmir is evident to all Kashmiris. It is heart wrenching to watch these corrupt officers making no effort to clean up, to attempt to provide somewhat better governance.

The other factor at play here is the fear factor. I had these conversations with Kashmiris from diverse background over the years, from government servants to clerics who give Friday sermons. I would always ask them: All that you say in public, do you believe in it? Most of them admitted in private that they do this venomous talking to insulate themselves from reprisal. I found that some of them even responded with a certain amount of shame. Personal remorse or not, all of them maintained that given the prevailing environment in Kashmir, they have no choice.

The only truth in Kashmir is the public sentiment against the state and its institutions. Anger among the common people is real, grievances are legitimate and wounds are both fresh and old. Rest everything is fake. Representation of the 'public sentiment' is fake. Swearing by the 'masla-e-Kashmir' by mullahs and vested interests are fake.

Thriving on Conflict Economy

Why is it fake? Because the so-called stakeholders are thriving on the conflict economy. They don't want an end to this business. Renowned historian Ramchandra Guha rightly observed that every stakeholder in Kashmir – be it India, Pakistan or the separatists – has blood on its hands.

Addressing a conference on Kashmir organised by Lehar in December 2016, former RAW chief AS Dulat said many youngsters in Kashmir thought that they now faced a 'do or die' situation. But the vast majority knows that this will not lead Kashmir anywhere. Dulat said it is tragic that the hopes of the average Kashmiris have been belied by India. And the separatists continue to give them false hopes that 'azadi ki subah jald tulu hogi' (the morning of freedom will soon rise for Kashmiris).

The Kashmir story has changed. Azadi has been replaced with 'Nizam-e-Mustafa'. There was a scope to contest the azadi narrative. But nothing can be said against the fresh narrative introduced zealously during this phase of violence. How can you be a Muslim and counter this narrative? This one is about faith. It has been imported from Pakistan's Jamaat-e-Islami. If you say no to it, you are an infidel and deserve to be killed. Under such a hostile and fearful environment, people are making adjustments. They are very vocal in public in support of the dominant narrative. In private, they have strong reservations about it.

In 2008, the High Court Bar Association, Srinagar, marched at Lal Chowk chanting '*Yehan kya chalega?*' A respected Bar member from the Sikh community was shouting along with his Muslim colleagues, 'Nizam-e-Mustafa'. I would never suggest that he was doing this for fear. No. He was simply siding with the dominant narrative.

Once I interviewed a certified Islamic jurist – a Mufti from south Kashmir. About the dominant narrative taking hold on Kashmir, he said, '*Jidhar ki hawa ho udhar ko chalein hum*'. I follow the breeze. I told him he was collaborating in the construction of a dangerous narrative, which could have serious consequences on the future of our coming generations. He replied, 'When Hafiz Saeed and Masood Azhar are equating the stone-pelters in Kashmir with *tauirana babeel,* how can I dare to disagree?' *Tauirana babeel* is a species of birds. The Quran says that when infidels were about to take control of Kaaba in Mecca, these birds dropped sand from the sky, killing the enemy army.

The narrative of 'Islam in danger' has been helped by BJP's polarisation politics in mainland India, which has further added to the insecurities of Kashmiris. But the seeds of the 'us and them' narrative was sown long ago. It seems that today, almost every section of Kashmir society is wittingly or unwittingly playing into the hands of the hardline religious extremists. Kashmir has witnessed a huge transformation from a secular, inclusive and pluralist society to one that is exclusive and intolerant. The Maududi sect of Islam is providing it the intellectual input.

No Space for Moderates

The majority non-Mullah population is providing the requisite human resource. The non-religious political organisations are finding themselves trapped in this situation. JKLF Chief, Yasin Malik, who is seen as moderate and secular, told a senior journalist from mainland India that there was no space now for secular politics in Kashmir. As a result, he too was realigning himself with the hardline Islamic ideology. The Wahabi and Maududi schools of thought have blurred the thin line between moderates and hardliners in the separatist camp. In addition, *Delhi has consistently done its bit in pushing the moderates to the wall.* Now, there is hardly anyone in Kashmir society who will dare to go against the tide and be left with any credibility.

There are two reasons for this. One, New Delhi has blocked all channels of communication with the moderates. It has stopped investing in the moderate section in the separatist camp. Two, the dominant narrative is driven by the Pakistan constituency in Kashmir. Nobody has the spine to challenge it. Some Kashmiris raise concern about the alarming rise of radical Islam in Kashmir. But they are living outside Kashmir. For the Kashmiris, especially the youth, this delegitimises their voice. Bereft of any logic, rationale or reason, Kashmiri youth is now greatly influenced by radical Islam. This has made it difficult for the silent older generation to debate the relevance of hardened narratives. Kashmir's intelligentsia has failed to rationalise the political ambitions of this vulnerable young generation.

The scope for reconciliation is steadily losing ground. In 2016, some Kashmiris started loudly contesting the romanticisation and glorification of militants. They soon quietened down because they could not garner any support, either from inside or outside. As for the Indian intelligentsia, the hardline sections of Kashmir civil society did not endorse their views. They discredited these voices by labeling them as Modi's aides. In January 2018, Lehar organised the second edition of the Chinar Dialogue in Srinagar. Our guests at the conference included noted journalists Siddharth Varadarajan and Shahid Siddiqui. Siddharth was labeled as Modi agent in Kashmir by a hawkish Kashmiri professor known for her extremist views. She vociferously stated at the conference that Kashmir does not follow Sufi Islam.

In 2015, renowned historian Ramchandra Guha had

delivered a lecture in Kashmir, where he had questioned the separatists for not fulfilling the expectations of Kashmiris. The next day, political commentators in Kashmir dubbed him as an agent of Hindutva. The atmosphere in Kashmir is so contaminated that it doesn't offer any choices. The mindset here is 'My way or the highway'. It is immaterial whether this is being done at the behest of the forces running the dominant narratives, or under the influence of the radical ideology.

I am particularly puzzled by the context of the religious extremism that we have been witnessing in Kashmir for many years.

What were the underlying factors responsible for the eruption of militancy in Kashmir? How far have we gone in pursuit of the resolution of that problem? The mobilisation around separatist sentiments did not begin with religion or language as the basis. The mobilisation began around the notion of *Kashmiriyat.* For yeons Kashmiriyat has always been perceived as the distinctly composite and essentially secular culture of the people here. This culture had evolved over centuries of coexistence and the confluence of Islam, Hinduism and Buddhism. The perception that this culture was in danger was ostensibly the spark that ignited the flame of discontent in the Valley.

It was in this context that in the beginning, Kashmiri Pandit leaders were seen sharing stage with the leaders of the Muslim community. The call was for preserving and protecting the unique identity of Kashmir, which was also guaranteed through a constitutional mechanism by the Union of India. But as the leadership of the movement passed on to bosses in Pakistan and their local representatives, a religious divide alien to the notion of Kashmiriyat crept in. *The syncretic Kashmiriyat was sacrificed at the altar of the imported jihad that had no base and no precedent in the life and culture of the people living in Kashmir.* In this way, Kashmiriyat, which is directly related to the idea of azadi, was demolished by leaders who swore to protect it.

Kashmir's tragedy is that as its leaders gave up on Kashmiriyat, they introduced the highly toxic extremist ideology, and are presently its vanguards. Now the vicious cycle is carrying on unabated with intellectual inputs from these leaders with extra-territorial ideologies. Innocent, gullible Kashmiri youth are the fodder which sustains this fire. Violence and counter-violence feed on each other, with the common Kashmiris trapped in this cycle. The breaking of this cycle of violence is a highly challenging task, given its inherent complexities.

The question is: Who will break this cycle?

Kashmir has hoped for reconciliatory politics from successive regimes in India and Pakistan. The perceived notion is that the 'Kashmir conflict' is the bone of contention between these two nation states. The resolution of this issue will open up new opportunities of growth and development in the region. Kashmir's society on one hand, and the Indian and Pakistani statecraft on the other hand, have witnessed structural and ideological overturns. These changes are an indicator that Kashmir is no more a bone of contention. It is now the 'conflict of convenience'.

Indian politics has witnessed a rightward shift. Kashmir has witnessed the transition from Kashmiriyat to Jihadi Islam. *Kashmir is now bigger than just being a contentious issue. It is being conveniently used locally and internationally by both India and Pakistan for their strategic gains.* The Kashmiris being consumed by this deadly conflict provide ladders to both countries to climb strategic heights. Select quarters in Kashmir are party to the strategic gains arising from the conflict. And sections of Kashmir society use this bloody conflict to secure a 'respectable' space in the society by conveniently striking the card of religious bigotry.

Understanding Between Mehbooba and Jamaat-e-Islami

INITIALLY WHEN I decided to write on how Mehbooba Mufti and Jamaat-e-Islami Kashmir are complimenting each other on the political landscape of Kashmir, I thought I would bring in the historical perspective of this relationship. At the time of writing, the State of Jammu and Kashmir was likely to go into election mode soon after the parliamentary elections. Understanding Mehbooba's political maneuvering helps us in understanding the deep relationship between the two. Since this is a sensitive issue, I have put my observations in a historical perspective to avoid any misinformation.

In the aftermath of the theft of the holy relic from the Hazratbal Shrine in 1964, Pandit Nehru removed Shamsud-Din from the post of Prime Minister of Jammu and Kashmir, and installed GM Sadiq as the first Chief Minister of the State.

On 31 March 1964, Sadiq announced that Sheikh Abdullah would be released from jail. On 8 April the Sheikh and 14 others including Mirza Afzal Beg were acquitted of the charges of sedition by a special court, which had been adjudicating the case since October 1958. Pandit Nehru simply apologised for casting doubts on Sheikh's loyalty to the Indian Union.

The charges of sedition, their subsequent withdrawal and release from jail – none of this impacted Sheikh's popularity. He emerged stronger than ever on the political landscape of Kashmir. Pandit Nehru sent Sheikh to Pakistan to persuade President Ayub Khan to start a dialogue process with India for the resolution of the Kashmir problem. Sheikh was warmly received in Rawalpindi. There was high excitement about his first visit to that country.

Ayub Khan accepted Sheikh's invitation to visit India to meet Pandit Nehru in June the same year. As Sheikh was readying to visit Muzafferabad, the news of Pandit Nehru's death reached him. He had to cut short his visit to return to Delhi.

Zulfikar Ali Bhutto travelled with Sheikh to Delhi for participation in Pandit Nehru's funeral. Sheikh's unprecedented clout disturbed his detractors, particularly the mullahs in Kashmir. Till his visit to Pakistan, Sheikh was considered the most popular leader in Jammu and Kashmir. After his maiden visit to Pakistan, he emerged as the best interlocutor. The leadership of both India and Pakistan were willing to rely on him.

Farooq Abdullah told me in December 2018 that the Pakistan administration had not been in favour of receiving the Shiekh in their country with such fervour, but judging the mood of the public, they were forced to do so. Moulvi Yusuf Shah, who had fled from Kashmir after the developments in October 1947, was the Sheikh's main detractor in Kashmir

Valley. After meeting Sheikh Abdullah in Rawalpindi, he expressed his desire to come back to Srinagar.

After Pandit Nehru's death, the leadership went into the hands of Lal Bahadur Shastri. According to Sheikh Muhammad Abdullah, Shastri was serious about resolving the Kashmir issue, but faced differences with his party colleagues regarding the modalities of the resolution process, particularly from Indira Gandhi.

Where did Pandit Nehru and Indira Gandhi differ in their approach to the Kashmir issue, and how did it impact Kashmir politics?

Nehru arrested Sheikh Abdullah in 1953 on the charges of sedition. He was primarily convinced by his advisors who were mostly Kashmiri pandits.

The Sheikh, soon after assuming charge, had abolished jagirdari and distributed the land to the poor peasants, who were Kashmiri Muslims. There were no ideological differences between Sheikh and Kashmiri Pandit leaders. Sheikh had chosen India over Pakistan by will and understanding.

Kashmiri Pandits and also the Hindu Mahasabha leaders were against the State's accession with the union of India. The Big Landed Estates Abolition Act 1950, spear-headed by Sheikh Abdullah, placed a ceiling on land ownership at 186 kanals (about 22 acres). The rest of the land of a landlord was redistributed among share-croppers and landless labourers, without any compensation to the landlord.

The land abolition law disturbed the Kashmiri Pandits and also the Kashmiri Mullahs, since both these categories were directly or indirectly beneficiaries of the Jagirdari nizam. After the Big Landed Estates Abolition Act was implemented in the State, the mullahs started hobnobbing with Liaquat Ali Khan and Kashmiri Pandits with Jawaharlal Nehru. In 1953, their common irritant, Sheikh Abdullah, was jailed on charges of sedition.

After his release from jail in 1964, Pandit Nehru reposed his trust in the Sheikh, and described his action of arresting him on charges of sedition in 1953 as most unfortunate.

Sheikh Abdullah held authority on both religious and political platforms in Kashmir. He had isolated the mullahs by empowering the common Kashmiris. Some mullahs who were in Indira Gandhi's coterie started advising her on how to dilute the authority – rather popularity of the Sheikh in Kashmir.

In February 1965, the Sheikh had gone to Mecca to perform Hajj. But before landing in Saudi Arabia, Sheikh accompanied by his wife and Mirza Muhammad Afzal Beg decided to visit some Islamic countries, Britian and France. I am not sure whether it was a coincidence or the meeting was advanced. Sheikh met Chinese Premier Chou en Lai in Algiers. What Sheikh wrote in his memoirs about this meeting is that they discussed China's agreement with Pakistan over Gilgit, part of the undivided erstwhile Jammu and Kashmir. Shiekh insists in his memoirs that he sent the summary of his conversation with the Chinese Premier to the Indian ambassador to China but Delhi was annoyed by the meeting.

He had also participated in the Islamic International Conference, where he stressed upon the need to promote Indian secularism. However, on his return to India Sheikh was arrested again and sent to Otacamund jail in Tamil Nadu. India and Pakistan went to war in 1965, followed by the Tashkent declaration in 1966.

Lal Bahadur Shastri and Ayub Khan reaffirmed their commitment to resolving the disputes between India and

Pakistan through peaceful means. Pertinently, they agreed to revert to their original position of 5 August 1965. Shastri died of cardiac arrest only hours after signing the Tashkent agreement, and Indira Gandhi occupied the office of the Prime Minister of India.

Indira released Sheikh from jail two years later, in 1968. As his statements indicate, Sheikh still had faith in the Indian democracy, but was live to the ground situation too. He was aware that the dishonesty, corruption and erosion of democratic institutions in Kashmir by the state had damaged the Indian cause in Kashmir, and there was much cynicism in the Valley. By this time it was clear that the one who was genuinely in India's favour was repeatedly jailed by the Indian government which lend its ears to caste elements instead.

Sheikh Abdullah's recognition of the ground situation was again projected as a conspiracy by both – Mullahs and Kashmiri Pandits in Delhi. A new scheme was hatched to dilute Sheikh's popularity.

By this time, Mufti Mohammad Sayeed was rising on the political landscape of Kashmir. After Mir Qasim, he was considered as the most powerful Congressman in Kashmir.

Indira Gandhi announced the dissolution of the Lok Sabha, and scheduled parliamentary elections in March 1971. Sheikh prevailed upon the leaders of the plebiscite front to participate in the elections. The local Congress leadership, which was now in the hands of mullahs, were against Sheikh's participation in the elections. They knew that winning the elections would be easy for Sheikh and his supporters in the plebiscite front.

Sheikh and Mirza Afzal Beg were in New Delhi. They were scheduled to leave for Srinagar on 8 January 1971 to formally announce their decision to participate in the elections. The flight which Sheikh and Beg were to board from New Delhi to Srinagar was cancelled on the pretext that a bomb had been discovered on it. Next day, both were debarred by the Centre from entering Jammu and Kashmir. Plebiscite Front was declared unlawful by the State assembly led by Sayed Mir Qasim.

Cunningness of the Congress Party

In the absence of a formidable opposition, the Congress party did well in parliament elections. *Mufti Sayeed convinced Indira to stop the Sheikh by invoking conspiracy theory again.*

Sheikh and Beg were still in exile. Mir Qasim and Mufti Mohammad Sayeed put forth an interesting proposal before Mrs Gandhi. The objective was to dilute Sheikh's authority on both religious and political platforms. *Jamaat-e-Islami, which was essentially a grouping of mullahs, was brought on board by Mir and Mufti to challenge Sheikh on both the fronts – political and religious. The argument put forth by Mir and Mufti was that weakening the Sheikh would strengthen the Congress in the Valley.*

Indira Gandhi agreed to the proposal and Mir Qasim and Mufti Sayeed entered into an arrangement with the mullahs in Jamaat-e-Islami. The ban on Plebiscite Front was still in place. *Mir Qasim went to elections in March 1972, giving five seats to Jamaat-e-Islami.*

This marked the end of the era of peasantry empowerment. *It was actually a class war, which the mullahs had lost with the rise of the Sheikh and his politics. They resurged in the early '70s, and again occupied center-stage on the political landscape in Kashmir. The understanding between the mullahs in Congress and Jamaat-e-Islami was a message which the common Kashmiris failed to read.*

With political empowerment offered on a platter by the

Congress and Mufti Mohammad Sayeed, Jamaat-e-Islami raised the banner of Maududi Islam in Kashmir. Mufti Sayeed continued to nurture the Jamaat to keep it on his side, with the political objective of weakening the Sheikh. *This saw the simultaneous disempowerment of Kashmir's peasantry and working class, who had been phenomenally empowered by Sheikh in a manner not seen anywhere in south-east Asia.*

Political Islam now enjoyed the patronage of the Congress, and by extension, state patronage in Kashmir. In 2010, a senior police officer in Kashmir asked me, 'Who is the ameer (president) of Jamaat-e-Islami Jammu and Kashmir?' We all knew the answer, so I found the question strange. 'Sheikh Ghulam Hasan', I responded. The police officer laughed. 'Since 1971, the ameer of Kashmir Jamaat is Mufti Mohammad Sayeed', he told me. I realised the full import of his words much later.

Rise of Jamaat in Kashmir

Pakistan was dismembered in 1971. Sheikh and his cohorts were facing both internal and external challenges. The defeat of Pakistan, the creation of Bangladesh and the emergence of Jamaat-e-Islami on the political landscape in Kashmir – all these impacted the future course of politics in Kashmir.

Pakistan lost the war in 1971. It also lost the vigour to push the Kashmir issue towards resolution. Instead, Pakistan clandestinely infused religion in Kashmir politics while the then ruling party in India overtly promoted the Jamaat.

What an interesting juncture for the Jamaat in Kashmir. It served Mufti Mohammad Sayeed's purpose and also of Pakistan. Jamaat's entry in Kashmir politics benefitted Mufti, helping him to erode the legitimacy of Sheikh Abdullah's National Conference. At the same time, the Jamaat still remains the most trusted ideological subsidiary of Pakistan in Kashmir.

Mufti Mohammed Sayeed and his daughter and political heir Mehbooba Mufti went close to the secessionist camp in Kashmir, with the assistance of the Jamaat. The regional and religious divide between Kashmir, Jammu and Ladakh reached their climax.

Meanwhile, with political empowerment, Jamaat-e-Islami succeeded in creating a huge network of madrasas in Kashmir, and infusing its narrow version of Islam upon a secular and tolerant populace.

Jamaat played this card very intelligently. In order to attract Kashmiri parents to admit their wards to their schools, Jamaat introduced the modern educational curriculum. Its cadre worked hard to ensure good results. Parents started admitting their children in the Jamaat-owned schools for competitive education. What they also got in the bargain was the Maududi version of Islam.

The campaign against the centuries-old tolerant, eclectic tradition that the Valley had inherited from Sufi saints was intensive and vicious. The plural, inclusive traditions of Kashmir were defenseless against this campaign. Though the State belatedly recognised the urgency for the revival of Sufi traditions in Kashmir, it went structurally wrong in achieving the desired results. *The Jamaat cadre labeled Sufis as India-sponsored culture. Its revival suffered a huge blow.*

Politics of deceit replaced Kashmir's value system. The mullahs, particularly Mufti Sayeed, carved out a strong space for himself on the political landscape of Kashmir by promoting the extremist version of Islam.

In June 1972, Sheikh and Beg were allowed to end their exile. Back home, Jamaat-e-Islami started a vicious and vociferous campaign against the Sheikh, questioning his Islamic credentials. Mosques were used for anti-Sheikh propaganda. Mufti Sayeed continued to build on Jamaat's anti-Sheikh rhetoric. Kashmir's real hero, Sheikh Abdullah, was projected as the villain, and was blamed for all the wrongs suffered by Kashmir. Syed Ali Geelani, who was the real collaborator in the Congress conspiracy against the Sheikh, started blaming him for abandoning the movement for right to self-determination.

These twin factors, the dismembering of Pakistan and *Jamaat-e-Islami's alliance with the Congress, r*esulted in the 1975 accord famously called the Indira-Abdullah accord or Beg-Parthasarthy accord.

Mehboob Beg, son of Mirza Afzal Beg, once narrated to me an incident. This speaks of how towering leaders of Kashmir were forced to change the goal post. 'After signing the accord on behalf of Sheikh Abdullah, when my father returned from Delhi to his Sarnal, Anantnag residence, he was confronted by a staunch Plebiscite Front worker Ismail Kak. On hearing about Beg Sahib's presence at the Sarnal residence, Ismail Kak came walking from Aishmuqam. On seeing my father, Ismail Kak started shouting that "you have sold us as well as your conscience to Delhi. You are traitors".

'Daddy kept telling him, "Ismail Kak please take some tea. Have you planted paddy in your fields?" Ismail Kak kept shouting about the "sell-off". Daddy continued with his question, "Have you planted paddy in your fields?" Angered by Daddy's response, Ismail Kak finally shouted, "How could I plant paddy in my fields when the Sha Khul (Martand canal) was breached above?"'

"Then what did you do?" asked my Dad. Ismail Kak furiously replied, "What do you expect, should I have left it barren? I plugged it again and sowed wheat and maize instead of rice. This was the only option left with me and other farmers in that area. We cultivate wheat and maize now."

'This was the response Daddy was waiting for. He shouted back at Ismail Kak, "Our Martand canal has been breached both in Pakistan and Kashmir. We also decided to cultivate maize and wheat (autonomy within the Union of India) and forget about cultivating paddy (self-determination)."'

Sheikh's popularity suffered a huge blow after the 1975 accord. He was elected as the leader of the Congress Legislature Party and sworn in as chief minister on 25 February 1975, after a gap of 22 years.[3]

Those who were collaborators for furthering the Congress agenda in Kashmir by discrediting Sheikh became leaders. The hero was marked as a villain during his final years, and also after his death. Congress politics in the late 1970s was guided by its all-out effort to keep the Left at bay all over India. In 1977 began the long Left rule in Bengal and Kerala. Sheikh Abdullah was leftish, liberal and progressive vis a vis the poor and landless.

My intention is not to hide the failures of Sheikh or the errors of his judgment. But the external and internal dynamics of Kashmir politics of his times are deliberately ignored, and he is blamed squarely for all the wrongs in Kashmir. Sheikh was angry with the leadership in New Delhi for eroding the special status of Jammu and Kashmir. How his detractors, particularly the Mullahs, were instrumental in the erosion of

3 There was Congress government headed by Mir Qasim in Jammu and Kashmir. After the Indira-Abdullah accord, Mir Qasim was told by the Congress high command to step down, pave way for the Sheikh to be the chief minister. Hence, Sheikh Abdullah was elected leader of Congress legislature party as NC had not fought this election.

the constitutional arrangement of Jammu and Kashmir with the Union of India is never discussed. The Sheikh's detractors changed the Valley's political narratives with ease.

Kashmir becomes a Political Pawn

In 1977, the Congress suffered a huge blow in the Parliament elections. Sheikh recommended the dissolution of the State assembly to go for fresh elections. Now the contest was direct. It was Congress and its subsidiary, the Jamaat-e-Islami on one side, and National Conference on the other side.

Janata Party, which was ruling at the Centre, also entered the fray. Maulana Masudi, a mullah, had been a life-long lieutenant of the Sheikh. Masudi and Mirwaiz Farooq fought the elections on Janata Party ticket. Sheikh returned to power with 47 seats. Even with his popularity at an all-time low, he won the majority in the State assembly. Out of 47 seats, Sheikh got 42 from Kashmir. Only three seats went to his opponents in Kashmir. The Congress drew a blank in Kashmir, and Jamaat got one – that of Syed Ali Geelani.

The Congress did not take the defeat in a positive spirit. Under the leadership of Mufti Mohammad Sayeed, it resorted to unrelenting political vendetta to dislodge Sheikh Abdulla. The Sheikh's health was deteriorating in these years. From 1977 to 1982, Sheikh Abdullah took a host of administrative measures to improve governance in Jammu and Kashmir. During this period, his focus was also on safeguarding his position, as there was disaffection within the National Conference cadre.

Through overt and covert means, Mufti tried to dislodge Sheikh. Mirza Afzal Beg engineered a defection in National Conference. Late in life, he had become ambitious about occupying the chair of chief minister. Kashmir saw the cobbling of an alliance between Beg's newly-formed Inquilabi National Conference, Janata Party, Congress and Mirwaiz Farooq. Opposite poles were coming together in Kashmir to dislodge Sheikh Abdullah.

With the death of Sheikh Abdullah in 1982, the politics of reason and rationale died in Kashmir. Now two extreme forces emerged on the political landscape of Kashmir: the secessionists and the unionists.

After Sheikh's death in September 1982, Mufti Mohammad Sayeed's target was Sheikh's son, Farooq Abdullah. In 1983, Farooq Abdullah got elected as chief minister after winning the elections with a thumping majority. Mufti constantly persuaded Indira Gandhi to remove Farooq by engineering defection in the National Conference. Indira agreed to Mufti's plans and appointed Jagmohan as the Governor of the State.

On 2 July 1984, Mufti finally succeeded in toppling the Farooq government by engineering defection. Governor Jagmohan swore in defected NC leader and Farooq's brother-in-law GM Shah as the new chief minister of Jammu and Kashmir with the support of the Congress party. Mufti's next plan was to replace GM Shah as chief minister. But the disenchantment and anger among the Kashmiri people against this government was growing. This forced Jagmohan to dismiss GM Shah on 7 March 1986.

By now, Rajiv Gandhi was the Prime Minister, and was also heading the Congress command. Realising the consequences of the blunder committed by his mother, Rajiv extended the hand of friendship towards Farooq. Under an interim arrangement, Farooq was sworn in again on 7 November 1986 as chief minister. Elections were held under the watch of Farooq's interim government in March 1987. The Congress was at last seeing sense.

A Snake in the Backyard

Mufti's political maneuvering in 1987 haunts Kashmir. The religio-political groups of Kashmir formed the Muslim United Front (MUF) and fought elections against the Rajiv-Farooq alliance. Jamaat was the essential component of MUF, and many other smaller groups and organisations were part of it. Mufti was morally and ethically bound to support the Rajiv-Farooq alliance but played double cross. In his election rallies, Mufti pointedly asked his supporters to vote for MUF candidates.

Farooq Abdullah had pointed towards Mufti's animosity towards him on many occasions. Were Mufti's actions driven by political rivalry? Was it animosity towards Farooq? Or was there more to it than met the eye?

It was Mufti Mohammad Sayeed who had brought Jamaat into election mode in 1972. Was that the reason that the Mufti supported MUF? Or was his plan to simply keep Farooq away from power?

In Mufti's home constituency of Bijbehara, Jamaat-e-Islami member Muhammad Sultan Bhat was pitched against NC candidate Abdul Gani Shah (Veeri). Mufti's workers voted for Jamaat-e-Islami's Muhammad Sultan. Nevertheless, Sultan lost the contest by a few votes because NC workers captured a couple of polling stations in Bijbehara town. Muhammad Sultan was from a peasant background. There was no resistance from Mufti's workers in Bijbehara to resist the booth-capturing by NC workers.

NC secured 36 seats and formed the government in Jammu and Kashmir with the support of the Congress party. MUF got four seats, including that of Syed Ali Geelani. I distinctly remember that soon after the elections, Mufti addressed a rally of his workers in Marhama village in Bijbehara constituency. He had a huge support base in his village.

Speaking at Marhama, Mufti was no more a secular Congress politician. He spoke about Islam and a caliphate. He invoked the son-in-law of the Prophet of Islam. I was a teenager then and attended the rally. I was surprised to hear Mufti speaking about Islam. Mufti had realised very early on that he could not reach the echelons of power as a Congressman. And he had envisioned how to capture power.

Soon, Mufti Mohammad Sayeed left the Congress. He joined VP Singh to form Jan Morcha in 1988. In Kashmir, Mufti brought in the Jan Morcha as the Awami Mahaz. Here he started his political journey on a different note. *His political and public meetings would start with the recitation of Quranic verses. In each public rally, he would invoke Islam in one way or the other.*

The enthusiastic MUF supporters, who got only four seats and believed that they could have fared better if the elections had been conducted in a free and fair manner, got disillusioned with the electoral process. Having little or no knowledge about how history had shaped Kashmir, these young MUF supporters drew conclusions without serious contemplation.

Without knowing the consequences of a violent movement, the handful of youth pushed Kashmir into an unending phase of bloody violence. Nobody approved the violence barring Syed Ali Geelani. What we know is that by then leaderless and directionless, young Kashmiris began to cross over to Pakistan Administered Kashmir for arms training. The violent phase of Kashmir's chequered history started in 1989.

In Delhi, VP Singh formed a coalition government. And his trusted ally, Mufti Mohammad Sayeed became the first

Muslim Home Minister of India. A popular saying goes, 'You can't keep snakes in your backyard and expect that they would bite your neighbours only'. Soon after assuming the charge of Home Ministry, Mufti Sayeed faced the biggest challenge of his life. His daughter Rubiya, a doctor, was kidnapped by Jammu Kashmir Liberation Front (JKLF) militants from Lal Ded Hospital in Srinagar in 1989.

The man who had sheltered the Jamaat for a good part of his political career was now begging for the life of his daughter.

JKLF was not a religious group. It was not a group controlled or conceived by mullahs either in Pakistan or in Kashmir. The JKLF militants only wanted their companions out of jail. Syed Ali Geelani had been preaching and teaching Islam all his life. When a journalist questioned him about Rubiya's kidnapping, he said, '*Behan apne bhaiyon ke paas hai. Koi galat baat nahi*'. This was a message to both sides. It was a reassurance to Mufti to relax. It was also a reminder to JKLF militants that they could not harm Rubiya Sayeed, daughter of Mufti.

The Killing Fields of the Nineties

On 14 August 1996, Advocate Muhammad Sultan Bhat, the local Jamaat leader from a remote village of Mufti's home constituency, was killed by government forces (a government led by President's Rule). His killing was a turning point in Mufti's political game-plan. The legislative elections were due in September that year. Mufti decided to field his daughter Mehbooba from Bijbehara against National Conference's Abdul Gani Veeri.

This is how the plan was hatched. Mufti summoned a meeting of local Jamaat workers of Bijbehara constituency and got their consent that they would vote and support Mehbooba.

Muhammad Sultan Bhat's entire family, which was still in grief and shock after his killing, nevertheless went to the polling booths to cast their votes in Mehbooba's favour. The voting pattern remained the same across Bijbehara constituency. *Mehbooba won, courtesy the Jamaat vote.*

Soon, Mehbooba resigned from both, the Congress party and the State assembly to form Peoples Democratic Party (PDP). Muzaffer Husain Beg, Ghulam Hasan Mir, Tariq Hameed Qara and BK Veshnavi were the founding members of the party. Mufti was seen consulting every known or unknown Jamaat member regarding future plans.

During the same time (during President's Rule), the Jamaat-e-Islami cadre was facing an intensive threat from government-sponsored renegades. These renegades were militants from non-Hizbul Mujahideen groups in the Valley. Their cadres had been crushed and slaughtered by Hizbul militants across the length and breadth of Kashmir. Jamaat cadres were providing inputs to Hizbul for killing the militants of other groups. Jamaat cadres would publicly announce that only the Hizbul militants had the right to live, and no other militants.

Even JKLF carders were slaughtered during this vicious campaign. These violent killings took place even within Srinagar city. Decaying bodies of militants affiliated to organisations other than Hizbul were commonly found in forests.

Jamaat cadres did not spare National Conference workers either. A shocking number of NC workers were killed by Hizbul militants at the behest of Jamaat members.

The killing of militants of rival groups by the Hizbul Mujahideen led to an internal conflict among militants. Hundreds of surviving militants surrendered before the government forces for protection. *Government forces (under*

President's Rule) used these surrendered militants against the Jamaat and Hizbul Mujahideen. The situation changed so rapidly that Jamaat cadres went into hiding in large numbers. Many of them migrated to Srinagar from rural areas to seek a safer environment.

The Trap

Mufti Mohammad Sayeed, meanwhile, continued his meetings with Jamaat workers in the process of forming his own party. In September 1999, Mufti sent me a message, asking me to see him at his Nowgam residence in Srinagar outskirts. I went the next morning. Mehbooba told me that Mufti had left for Delhi. He had issued strict instructions that I must stay at his Nowgam residence till he returned from Delhi.

Mehbooba took me to the kitchen. In Kashmiri homes, it is common to sit and eat in the kitchen. As she opened the door, I was stunned to see a dreaded Hizbul militant, Amin Baba. He was the divisional commander for south Kashmir, and hailed from Bijbehara, Mufti's hometown.

Amin Baba was sitting comfortably in the kitchen, sipping noon chai – the salt tea favoured by Kashmiris. It was such an unexpected contact with the dreaded militant that I was terror-struck. I felt as if my legs were stuck in quicksand.

In 1999, when I was in her house, I told Mehbooba that I would stay back in Srinagar with a relative till Mufti returned from Delhi. When I learnt that Mufti was back, I went to see him. In the lawns of Mufti's residence, I saw a gentleman strolling about at ease. When I saw his face, I could not believe my eyes. It was Farooq Lasoo, a militant from Khiram, a village in Mufti's home constituency. Now I could understand what was going on.

Mufti founded the People's Democratic Party (PDP)

in 1999. The same year, he offered me the PDP ticket from Bijbehara assembly segment, from where Mehbooba had resigned. Elections in Bijbehara were scheduled to be held along with Parliament elections, which were due in October. There were several aspirants for the PDP ticket. Mufti wanted to give it to me because I was the son-in-law of the deceased Jamaat leader, Muhammad Sultan Bhat.

I told Mufti that I should consult my parents before saying yes. He cautioned me that this was a golden opportunity. I should not miss it by seeking consent from parents or friends. Ill luck as it was, I went back to my village and sought permission from my family members to contest the elections.

No sooner than I asked for their permission, my three brothers, cousin, father and uncle were so enraged that they started beating me with whatever they could lay their hands on. So sever was their chastisement that my left shoulder got dislocated. Somehow, I managed to jump out of the window to save myself. My wife went on a hunger strike and took a glass of water after five days, when I promised her that I would not contest.

I was Mufti's choice, courtesy my father-in-law. I had a strong Jamaat background. There were some lawyers and senior political workers who were strong aspirants, but Mufti rejected them all.

Don't Worry, Hizbul Brothers

Soon after the formation of PDP, Mehbooba got in touch with almost all local Hizbul commanders through the Jamaat cadre. She developed her own network among them through her pointsmen. A senior police officer, again a mullah, also provided her links with the militants.

After forming the government in 2002, a huge public meeting

addressed by Mehbooba in Ganderbal in central Kashmir became front page news. At this rally, Mehbooba told militants that they need not worry, as PDP represented them now.

In the year 2000, Mehbooba facilitated the exfiltration of Ghulam Nabi Khan alias Amir Khan, a top Hizbul commander, to Pakistan. Amir Khan was made the chief commander of Hizbul in Pakistan after the fall of Ahsan Dar.

Later, in 2005, Amin Baba alias Abid had crossed over to Pakistan through the Wagah border in a security jeep that belonged to Mubarak Gul, a former NC legislator. Gul was later arrested. Amin's passport had been arranged by Mehbooba, with her father as then chief minister. Gul had picked up Amin Baba from the residence of Mufti Mohammad's younger brother Mufti Amin. He had reportedly been hiding there for six months till his passport was made.

Jamaat had suspended its activities after 1991. After Mufti's ascent to power, Jamaat got the returns. It was allowed by Mufti to revive and reorganise its cadre. During 1998-99, the Jamaat leadership developed links with the intelligence agencies through Mufti and then Ameer-e-Jamaat, GM Bhat, and reached an agreement with the PDP government.

I wanted to know from AS Dulat, then in-charge of the Kashmir desk in the then Prime Minister Atal Bihari Vajpayee's office, about the contact between Jamaat-e-Islami leaders and the intelligence agencies. Dulat told me that he had met GM Bhat a number of times. According to Dulat, GM Bhat was a gentleman and he would often meet him. However, Dulat was not sure about the secret deal between the Jamaat and the establishment. 'I was in Prime Ministers office then, may be the deal might have been reached by the appropriate people', Dulat told me. When I reminded Dulat of a speech Bhat had given to his members in Srinagar in the year 2001 wherein he asked his cadre to 'reveal your identity to the army guys whenever and wherever you confront them, you will be safe', Dulat said may be the deal must have happened between the Indian army and Bhat. However, the common thread in either case remains Mufti Mohammad Sayeed.

The agreement was that Jamaat cadres would not be targeted by the government forces henceforth. They were free to restart their organisational activities with certain riders. The conditions were that no Jamaat leader would talk about Caliphate, they would support Mufti in the 2002 elections, and Jamaat would directly enter into electoral process later.

In 2010

In the 2010 uprising in Kashmir which cost many young lives, Mehbooba's role was that of a highly combustible agent. She did everything to keep Kashmir boiling in order to dislodge Omar Abdullah of the NC, who had succeeded Mufti in 2008 elections as Chief Minister. Mufti himself would monitor the situation with great excitement. He would be very bothered on a day which passed without any causality. I am personally witness to it that Mufti would get irritated if someone told him that the agitation would die, and Omar would survive.

Mufti was content to see the *hartal* calendar issued by Geelani going strong. With this calendar, the agitations and hence the casualties continued. In October 2010, I got a call from SSP SBK Riyaz Bedar to see him at his office at the CID headquarters in Srinagar. There was tight curfew in the city. He sent an inspector in civil clothes to pick me up on a motorbike from my rented house in the outskirts of Srinagar.

Bedar took me to IGP (CID) S Srinivas, where the duo

asked me for help. I was wondering how I could help them. Here goes the story.

Some senior separatist had gone to Mufti's residence on Gupkar Road at night on 26 September. Srinivas and Bedar said *there were differing inputs from intelligence sources as to who was the separatist.*

The duo was under the impression that I was still close to Mufti and his companion and joined him regularly during evening walk. Hence, they felt I could ascertain the truth. They did not know that I had left Mufti three months ago. I had protested strongly before both Mufti and Mehbooba that they were using violence as a tool to dislodge Omar. And I parted ways with them.

It was interesting to know from Srinivas and Bedar about a senior separatist's visit. After 15 days of working hard to reach the truth, it was established that Geelani had visited the Muftis on that night.

Mehbooba once called me and asked me to provide the mobile number of a youth PDP worker of Anantng, Bilal Ahmad Najar. I had been informed by an officer of SP rank in Anantnag that Bilal was creating law-and-order problems in the town and organising stone-pelters. Bilal had recently got married. I summoned him and cautioned him that he was on the radar of the security forces (it was Omar Abdullah's government at this time) and should go into hiding. I told him to take his wife along and stay in Jammu for some time.

The situation improved in Anantnag after Bilal's exit. The intensity of violent protests went down. Mehbooba called me and asked me for Bilal's number, which I said, I did not have. She somehow got his number. I do not know what transpired between them. On 20 September, I was at my house in Srinagar when I received the news that Bilal had been critically injured in police firing.

I rushed to SMHS Hospital where some youth from Anantnag started crying on seeing me. Pained at Bilal's fate, I shouted at them, 'Go and mourn at Mehbooba's residence. You provided his contact number to Mehbooba, who brought him back from Jammu to die.'

Mehbooba continued to engineer the protests even after the situation seemed to be easing. She was there to see that the agitations didn't fizzle out, with the desired results of Omar resigning as chief minister. In 2016 and 2017, Mehbooba faced what she had sown for Omar in 2010.

In 2019

Before the 2019 assembly elections in Kashmir, predictably, Mehbooba has successfully revived her contacts with the Jamaat cadres. The present Ameer-e-Jamaat does not seem to have full knowledge of how Jamaat has become very close to Indian intelligence agencies. But he was elected by majority vote. Fayaz won 79 votes out of total 160 votes that were cast. Ghulam Muhammad Bhat, who was instrumental in reviving the Jamaat, got 35 votes.

Jamaat-e-Islami and its Falah-e-Aam Trust (an educational trust) has been receiving money from across the border since decades. Intelligence inputs suggest that one Sona Ullah Dar – who exfiltrated to the other side in the 1990s – was the hawala handler for Jamaat. Bhat had been the president of the organisation from 1985 to 88,1997 to 2000 and in 2000 to 2003 and 2015 to 2018. Bhat also headed Falah-e-Aam Trust for a good period of time. So, the Intelligence agencies suggest that the hawala handler Sona Ullah Dar was very close to Bhat. However, of late, Bhat was very keen to see the transactions happening through his son based in the Gulf. This irritated

Dar, who reportedly enjoys clout with the Pakistani deep state and militant outfits. I was told by a senior intelligence officer that it was Dar who saw to it that Bhat is not re-elected as Jamaat president in Indian Kashmir. Some Jamaat insiders even say that a diatribe was unleashed against Bhat, accusing him of being close to Indian Intelligence agencies, in order to create a case against Bhat. The trick worked and Bhat was succeeded by Fayaz Ahmad Sheikh, a die-hard Maududi *bhakt*.

Mehbooba has revived her soft separatism politics and is presently visiting the families of slain militants. Hizbul commander Riyaz Naikoo has asked the families of militants not to allow Mehbooba to visit them. Let us see how things shape up in the coming months.

Role of Jamaat-e-Islami in Building Kashmir's Radical Narrative

IN THE previous chapters, how Jamaat-e-Islami emerged on the political landscape of Kashmir has been discussed, and how it entered into a secret deal with the intelligence agencies to save its cadres from the onslaught of renegades in the mid-90s. Mufti's People's Democratic Party and the state agencies in New Delhi had two aims vis-à-vis the Jamaat.

Mufti had mastered the skill of using the Jamaat as a ladder for his ambitions. The State agencies gave breathing space to the Jamaat on the commitment that it would finally join the electoral process. So, who got the best deal? PDP, Delhi or the Jamaat?

From 2002 onwards, when the Jamaat was accidentally headed by non-mullahs, it tried to open up a debate within its cadres about the option of entering the electoral process in Kashmir. But its leadership was too guarded to give a clear direction to this debate. Was this debate initiated intentionally to befool the people in Delhi? Or were the Jamaat leaders burdened under the dominant narrative (Islam) which their organisation had nurtured ideologically in Kashmir?

One cannot be sure of answers to these questions. But a change was visible on the ground. From 1999 onwards, the Jamaat cadres *would not* invoke the Kashmir issue. The Jamaat leadership put the 'Kashmir conflict' low in their list of priorities. They gave the impression that they were only remotely concerned about politics. The Jamaat leadership ensured that the Kashmir desk in Delhi should feel relaxed. I believe they succeeded in achieving this.

New Delhi's Kashmir Desk seemed to go into sleeping mode where the Jamaat was concerned. Back home, Mufti provided every logistic support to the radical Jamaat for its revival. Jamaat utilised this time to reorganise its cadres. It enjoyed complete freedom in infusing its orthodox version of Islam among the youth in Kashmir.

When Jamaat organised its first annual congregation in Kulgam district in 2005, it was like a tsunami. Everybody from Srinagar to New Delhi was surprised to see the show of strength. I was amazed to see the level of participation of youth in this annual congregation. Soon after this congregation in south Kashmir, youth influenced by Jamaat ideology created social networking platforms in abundance and posted whatever content they pleased online. It was clear now that Jamaat's so-called 'surrender policy' to the Indian intelligence forces had brought it far greater returns than the returns accrued by Delhi.

But Mufti, the wily politician, got the best deal of his life. New Delhi erroneously believed that jihadism could be curbed by separating Jamaat from Hizbul and sparing it. *Delhi failed in its assessment of Jamaat's surrender policy.* Giving a long rope to the Jamaat may have been a diplomatic or tactical move on the part of New Delhi. But this should have been coupled with addressing the alienation of Kashmiris, which still provides pastures for extremist ideologies.

Was Mufti's healing-touch policy conceptualised to address the issue of alienation? Did it work at ground level? One can debate these questions. The bigger issue before the Indian state is that the present phase of violence in Kashmir is beyond the narratives of azadi and separation from India. Jamaat has very intelligently indoctrinated Kashmiri youth with its narrow, conservative worldview.

Jamaat becomes Mainstream

In a large measure, this has been achieved through the schools run by Falah-e-Aam trust of Jamaat, which were opened in hundreds. Jamaat created infrastructure worth millions across Jammu and Kashmir. It purchased land in the outskirts of Jammu at Beli Charana and Sidrah, and handed it over to its office-bearers for constructing houses. In Kashmir, the head-office of Falah-e-Aam Trust and the residential complexes of its office-bearers are situated at Nowgam bypass, next to Mufti's private residence.

Jamaat enjoyed the status of a mainstream party in Kashmir after its 'surrender' policy. It remained at the forefront in destroying Kashmir's centuries-old pluralistic, inclusive and eclectic culture by infusing its radicalised worldview. Jamaat's access to the power centers in Kashmir can be compared to that of the Wahabis in Saudi Arabia.

Kashmir's present violent phase is less about grievances that we read about often in the writings of the Delhi media. I wonder if the situation in Kashmir will improve even if the Indian government negotiates autonomy with the Kashmiri leadership, and even if it grants autonomy to Kashmir and restores the 1953 Delhi agreement in letter and spirit.

The ideology which now sweeps over Kashmir has originated from the Maududi version of Islam. It synchronises with the deadliest ideologies across the world. A few hundred militants don't pose a threat to humankind. *The challenge we face is the militant mindset* emerging from the domain of ideas imported from radical Islamists, particularly Maududi and Syed Qutb.

I was not surprised on watching a video on social media in which a group of Kashmir university students and teachers offer prayers for Egypt's ousted Islamist president Muhammad Mursi who died after collapsing in a court on 17 June. Jamaat-e-Islami of Maududi and Ikhwan-ul-Muslimeen of Sayed Qutub are two sides of the same coin. They are ideological cousins.

Online radicalisation has taken precedence in Kashmir over person-to-person indoctrination as the millennium moves to its third decade. The non-violent creed of Islamic extremism has gained a strong foothold in paradise with the Jamaat's unrelenting pursuit of this objective, and Mufti's patronage. Delhi is unaware of the gravity of the situation in Kashmir. Ideological fodder is available to the violent creed in abundance. This is why militants find it easy to recruit youth from Kashmir in their cadres.

The youth who rush to 'encounter sites' to give safe passage to holed-up militants are swept up by the same ideological fervour. It can be argued that Kashmiris are fighting, and not just resisting 'Indian oppression'. It is not that simple. *Every sane voice that rises against this violent form of Islam is silenced forever. No one can raise his voice against the Islamists, the perpetrators of violence. But everyone is free to curse the Indian state.* Killings on the basis of political affiliations and on mere suspicion are justified by the Jamaat cadres in every nook and corner of Kashmir Valley. Some Jamaat workers even issue decrees declaring the victims as apostates.

Killing of apostates (in Kashmir, it's those who don't accept the violent form of Islam) is a major argument forwarded by the Jamaat in Jammu and Kashmir. In May 2015, the Ahmadi sect planned a peace conference in Srinagar. Mullahs and Jamaatis were infuriated. In every mosque of Kashmir Valley, Jamaat cadres and mullahs warned the government of serious consequences if the conference was allowed to happen. That was my first day on Twitter. I tweeted, tagging Mirwaiz Umer Farooq, to differentiate between a state ruled by Islamic shariah and a Muslim-majority state.

The state of Jammu and Kashmir has its own Constitution. Everybody is free to practice or preach his religion or faith. Everyone is equal before the law. How can one deny a particular sect from following its belief? The Mirwaiz was among those who warned the government (Mufti-led) several times during that period. The result was that the government didn't allow Ahmadis to hold their conference. Yet, this Kashmir does not follow Sharia and is believed to be governed by Indian laws.

There are hundreds of such incidents where the perpetrators of the violence are the Islamic militia. But *the affected individual or the victim's family blames the security forces in order to avoid further attacks at the hands of militants.* The Jamaat and the separatists have developed vicious propaganda machineries and no time is wasted in blaming the Indian security forces for the heinous crimes committed by the militants.

Kashmir's media is an equal participant in this game. It does not dare to name the perpetrators of violence if they are militants. But it loses no time in raising the pitch if the crime is committed by Indian security forces.

In May 2018, three civilians were killed by militants in Sopore market in broad daylight. People identified the militants, but Kashmir's media did not name anyone. The news reports carried by almost all newspapers said that 'unidentified' gunmen killed three civilians in Sopore.

After the exodus of Kashmiri Pandits, Kashmir's society is largely homogenous. With Muslims all around, the extremist ideology finds it easy to influence the populace. It is Kashmir's peculiar situation that gaining a foothold in the minds of its people, especially the young, is not possible by talking about the value system or the traditions that we followed for centuries. You have to compete in toxicity, otherwise you will be discredited – as happened with the Sufis. Although all religious groups are competing with each other in strengthening their hold on Kashmir, there are very few success stories.

The competition in spreading toxicity has reached a point where religious groups are resorting to cultural aggression to prove their loyalty. The clerics take refuge in *Iqbayaat* and Urdu literature. *The traditional Kashmiri attire is being replaced by Arabic gowns and turbans to appear highly religious, cultured and sophisticated.*

Since Maududi can't be the uniting force for different schools of thought in Kashmir, Pakistan's national poet Iqbal – who is owned by one and all – and his couplets are central to raise passion for jihad in Kashmir. Iqbal is acceptable to all schools of thought in Kashmir, for he is known for engendering

Islamism among Muslim youth and ridiculing democracy. His couplets are on the lips of every Jamaati. We now see people from other schools of thought like Deobandis, Tabhleegis and Wahabi regard Iqbal as the emotional and ideological fountainhead of political Islam for arousing passion for jihad and challenging the state.

The pattern of messaging on social networking in Kashmir has shown us that Iqbal's poetry is the centrifugal force in arousing passions. Examine the content of theology being taught in the mushrooming madrasas of various sects in Kashmir. The Wahabis, Tablighees and Jamaatis are competing in establishing madrasas and attracting children from marginalised communities.

The Text Changes

The text of Islamic studies has changed drastically since 2004. Earlier, the thrust was on personal purification. Now the focus is on exhibitionist Islam. Kashmiri customs and rituals have been replaced by Arabic culture and mannerisms. The conversational nuances, greetings, colloquialisms and invocations are Islamic and not Kashmiri. Religious bigotry and obscurantist texts in these madrasas are creating a generation of semi-literate youth who identify themselves more with Islam than with Kashmir society.

The theology of thought control has worked. The 'us versus them' theory works in two dimensions – internal and external. If you don't agree with them, you are an apostate and hence against them – even if you are a Muslim. Externally, people of other religions are 'enemies'. The all-pervasive slogan about the ideology of Jamaat and other religious groups which echoes everywhere in Kashmir is this: *Azadi ka matlab kya? La illaha illallah.* This has become the rallying cry of the campaign to totally Islamise Kashmir society.

The seeds of distortion of Kashmir's history and the dominance of Sunni religious dogma were sown with the advent of Jamaat-e-Islami in Kashmir. These seeds have blossomed. Ahmadis are forcibly converted in habitations where their presence is miniscule. In my village in south Kashmir, there were two Ahmadi families. Abdul Ahad Khan was a X-Ray technician who served the people of the village all his life. He would take patients from his village to wherever he was posted for treatment and diagnosis. Khan died in 2006. He was buried in a local graveyard.

The local Jamaat unit protested against his burial and demanded the removal of his body. All those who participated in his funeral prayers were asked to perform nikah with their wives again. According to the Jamaatis, the nikah had ceased upon offering prayers for an Ahmadi.

The onslaught didn't stop here. Abdul's son, Farooq Ahmad Khan, a law graduate, was threatened with social boycott if he did not convert.

Witness the drama that unfolded now. Jamaatis called Farooq to a mosque, read the Kalima and converted him. The next day, Deobandis too summoned Farooq, claiming that only they can certify his conversion. Farooq again did whatever he was asked to. Next year in winter, he was summoned by both the sects again to certify his conversion.

An Islamic Caliphate in Kashmir

There are thousands of unregulated madrasas whose curriculum is never discussed or examined. They are free to teach their own Islamist and jihadist lessons, leading to hate campaigns against infidels and apostates. These madrasas not only engender conservatism but have emerged as hate centers. *Kashmir is now witnessing the rise of a new generation of extremists.* They are motivated by the ideology of conservatism locally. They do not need to go to Pakistan, as was the case earlier. We have home-grown jihadists now, courtesy Jamaat-e-Islami and its political mentors providing them asylum. These youth fight alongside the militants.

Zakir Musa or Riyaz Naikoo speaking about establishing the Islamic caliphate in Kashmir is not an issue to be seen in isolation. *They reflected the ground situation in Kashmir.* It is not the madrasas or Jamaat alone who provide ideological input to extremism in Kashmir. Educationists, teachers, media-persons – there are many who preach and promote toxic extremist ideology.

I am not surprised to see educated Kashmiri youth joining militant ranks. A major factor is the environment in Kashmir's government or semi-government educational institutions where the youth secure degrees. Religion has taken precedence over everything in our colleges and universities. Elitist ideologues of extremist ideology, who are present in universities and colleges, are vital links in promoting these ideologies. During the 2016 uprising, I personally witnessed a group of teachers in Kashmir University promoting unrest on the campus.

How the political class is exploiting this situation needs to be examined. In March 2018, South Kashmir Civil Society, a group of retired government servants involved in literary activities convened a meeting. I was also invited. The meeting was scheduled at the government rest house in Qazigund on the Srinagar-Jammu National Highway. I drove from Srinagar to Qazigund.

As I was interacting with the hosts, one more guest dropped in. He was wearing a white gown, had tied a white turban, and had a long white beard. I was scared by his attire and looks. I shared my fears with the organiser, who laughed. We all went to the meeting hall. This gentleman was given much more respect and visibility, compared to others. I learnt that he is a doctor. Many people suffering from hypertension visit him.

He started his speech with Quranic verses and recited a couplet by Iqbal. Then he said, 'We must participate in the elections on one point – to establish Nizam-e-Mustafa (Islamic rule). This is the only solution to all the problems we are facing in Kashmir.' A young man sitting by my side interrupted the doctor and said that the state comprises of three distinct regions, which follow different religions. Then how was it possible to establish the caliphate, the man asked. The doctor was unperturbed. 'We need not establish it now', he said. 'We can defer it for another 50 to 60 years till the situation becomes ripe for its establishment', he said. He possibly had his long-term plan well in place and working.

This is what the political class in Kashmir is doing. No one is bothered about the implications of what they promote. The separatist camp claims to represent the sentiment of the people of Kashmir. I completely disagree, they only exploit the sentiment to their advantage. They do not have the spine to convey to people that emotions should match the collective wisdom based on rationality and logic. In absence of reason and rationality emotions only make beasts out of humans.

Take for instance the mad action of our emotional youth of rushing to encounter sites. It is a forgone conclusion that the one who comes in the line of fire may be killed. But the youth continue with this foolhardy action, following emotional outbursts. Do our politicians ask these youth not to venture close to encounter sites, since it is dangerous? But every politician wails and mourns over a 'civilian casualty'.

Imagine how insidious the invasion is. A writer used to call me frequently without any sense of timing. He would start long and boring conversations, and always ask one thing,'What is our role as the civil society in breaking this deadlock?' I evaded his question for many days. One day, he called me about 20 times. It irritated me. 'What can be our role?' he asked again. I posed a counter-question. 'What do you stand for?' He started meandering, but I cut him short and retorted, 'Listen, if you are for the Islamic state, Geelani is there. If you are for azadi, Yasin Malik is there. If you are for right to self-determination or its cousin, Mirwaiz is there. If you seek autonomy, Dr Farooq is there. If you like self-rule, Mehbooba represents it. Where is the role coming for you? If you stand for one or the other proposed roadmap, go and follow anyone among them.'

Politics in Kashmir is as tangled as the conflict itself. There are several groups other than the separatists who speak in the same language as Geelani, Malik or Mirwaiz. Yet, they claim to be independent entities.

The so-called intellectual class in Kashmir is keen to be relevant. But they are equally weak in floating new ideas because of fear factor or love for money. This silent approval for extremist politics is dangerous for Kashmiri society as a whole. Living in the shadow of guns and stones, there is no scope for speaking your heart and mind in Kashmir.

If Kashmir's intelligentsia keeps hiding behind these hardened narratives, Kashmir will turn into Afghanistan. *Going against the wind needs courage, which has become the biggest causality in Kashmir.* The elites have secured the future of their children. They are quietly watching the dance of death in Kashmir's streets as if it is a soap opera.

As for the common Kashmiris, the father is more radicalised

than the son. The mother is resorting to chest-beating in street protests, and the children are watching it all with enthusiasm. Romanticisation and glorification of militants is indoctrinating children in their homes.

One of my elder brothers has a son and three daughters. In 2016, he would take his son with him for stone-pelting. Who will he blame if one day his son is caught in cross-firing during an encounter? No one in our village told him that he was inviting death to his house. Instead, people would make a hero of him, and many men of our area followed him in doing the same.

Extremist ideologies have seeped deep into Kashmir's homogenous society. Sitting in cosy armchairs far from Kashmir, few are willing to admit it. Every single individual who matters or who could have made some difference is conveniently allowing the situation to drift further right.

Failure is India's

Kashmir watchers outside Kashmir are as insensitive as separatists when it comes to understanding the present phase of bloody violence. *The root cause, of course, is the insensitivity on part of the Indian government. Owing to this insensitivity, it has failed to win Kashmiris back for decades. The actions of the Indian government have consistently alienated the people of Kashmir.*

But today, the situation in Kashmir is far beyond grievances or political reach-out. It is an altogether different society now – radically indoctrinated, fundamentally extremist and politically Islamist. Even if India succeeds in disengaging Pakistan from Kashmir, the situation may remain the same, I am afraid.

The radical jihadist is now home-grown. The power corridors in New Delhi must understand and diagnose the problem in order to frame appropriate responses. The rallying point common among all schools of thoughts in Kashmir is the narrative of 'Muslim victimhood'. This is the most dangerous weapon that the Kashmiris are armed with. *The Government of India will have to understand and devise a strategy to remove this 'Muslim victimhood' narrative with compassion and wisdom.*

The Double Dealers of Kashmir

AS I was preparing to write on this subject, the news of 2009 IAS topper Shah Faesal resigning from the administrative services came in. The reaction on social media sites followed fast. Kashmiris hurling abuses at him on Facebook didn't surprise me. There is a strong social networking of extremists in Kashmir, who don't waste time in denigrating and demeaning a person inclined towards mainstream politics. What came as a shock to me was the Facebook post of a retired government servant, Farooq Renzu Shah. He wrote, 'Shah Faesal will get 90% votes if he contests on behalf of victims of Kashmir, he will lose deposit if contests on behalf of killers'.

This gentleman rose to the position of Secretary to the J&K government. He served as Director Information and Public Relations. He had the blessings of Farooq Abdullah.

Omar Abdullah also trusted him. Ghulam Nabi Azad as Chief Minister did not dislocate him, for the gentleman was considered loyal to the chair, and would do everything to keep his masters happy.

In 2010, the Speaker of the Legislative Assembly M Akbar Lone annoyed media-persons sitting in the media gallery. I was working for a local newspaper then. Two women journalists were sitting on my left. I suggested that we should boycott the proceedings till the Speaker apologised for his unparliamentary remarks. The word spread, and within no time the media gallery was deserted. The friction continued for several days.

Shah was Director, Information then. He literally begged us to resume the coverage of the ensuing session of State legislature. If this gentleman smelt that any newspaper or news agency was going to write something against the government, he would appear in the office of that newspaper at late night hours and ensure that nothing wrong was printed.

The Sold-out Media

In the 2016 uprising, militants celebrated Pakistan Independence Day on 14 August at many places in the Valley by hoisting the Pakistan flag and firing gunshots as celebration. It was expected that the news would appear in the newspapers the next day, on 15 August.

On August 22, I was reading Kashmir's largest circulated English daily, when I was startled by what I saw on the last page. It carried a huge photograph on the top showing militants hoisting the Pakistan flag. The caption below was even more surprising. It said, 'Militants hoisting Pakistani flag in a Kulgam village'. I had seen this flag-hoisting live in Redwani village of Kulgam District on August 14. A few hundred jubilant youth were shouting slogans when militants hoisted the flag and fired gunshots in the air. *Why was the newspaper carrying the huge photograph on August 22? One, more adventurous enthusiastic emotional youth would aspire for a misadventure like this – Pakistan, separatists happy. Two, establishment happy over delayed photograph.*

There are many double-dealers in Kashmir, and Kashmir press is no exception. There are editors and owners who strive hard to sustain their publications. They are always seen moving from one office to another to get advertisement business to sustain their publication.

On the other hand many in Kashmir media are now entrepreneurs, not journalists. They have destroyed Kashmir for money. They take money from Pakistan and also from India. Their palms are greased by the government set-up and also the separatists. They consistently and constantly play out the monochromatic narrative of 'victimhood' and conveniently avoid reporting on extremist provocations. Without any fear of contradiction, I would like to write with full responsibility that Kashmir media is as biased as prime time news channels like *Republic, Times Now* and *Zee News*. The militarised coverage by Prime-Time News alienates Kashmiris from the Indian mainland while the separatist outlook of Kashmir media is a grand source of instigation.

Second important point regarding Kashmir media is its complexion. Look at the number of elitist mullahs working for both local and national media. Bukharis, Geelanis, Andrabis, Makhdoomis, Masoodis, Muftis, Shahs, Peerzadas , so on and so forth. As mentioned earlier in the book, mullahs constitute just 3% of Kashmir's population but they control the levers of both government and non-government institutions, particularly the media.

As for the field reporters, they are mostly from the majority community. Young and unexposed to the outer-world, these hardly understand the nuances of Kashmir politics. They get swayed by emotions. They come from the same society which is perpetually high on emotions.

These reporters are not mature enough to appreciate that rising passions can lead to further human losses. They have a responsibility to stop this vicious circle of death which consumes only Dars, Rathers, Bhats, Wanis, Mirs, Tantrays, Ganais, Sheikhs etc. They are yet to realise that Bukharis, Makhdoomis, Geelanis, Naqshbandis, Muftis, Shahs appear on prime time for chest-beating. But the kin of these elitist mediapersons are not seen stoning or protesting in the streets.

I had arguments with Shujaat Bukhari on several occasions in Delhi and elsewhere. I would always express my resentment over his double standards. How could he and others like him raise the pitch for emotional outburst regarding Kashmir when none from their elitist clan is seen protesting in the streets or rushing to the encounter sites.

Why is it that children of non-mullahs are prone to taking up arms? Children of mullahs take up plum jobs in Kashmir in almost all institutions, while children of poor farmers die on the streets for the 'noble cause of Kashmir's liberation'.

Basharat Bukhari, the elder brother of Shujaat Bukhari, left PDP and joined NC. Suhail Bukhari, a close relative of Basharat, joined PDP. Now, the fight in Sangrama constituency in Baramulla will be between two Bukharis, and one of them will win. What is the population of Bukharis in Sangrama constituency? Less than one per cent.

Many people in Delhi including senior journalists, politicians and civil society members often ask me why was south Kashmir on the boil? I told them it was because Mehbooba was ruling over the majority through the minority.

It was the common voter in south Kashmir who voted Mehbooba to power. Bhat, Dar, Lone, Mir, Tantray, Turray, Sheikh, Ganai, Kumar, Sofi – these and other common Kashmiris were the ones who voted for her in large numbers. But those who secured appointments were the Bukharis, Shahs, Andrabis, Hamdanis. Mullahs who retired were rehabilitated politically. They manned public-sector undertakings and grabbed prize postings in every department.

Even MLAs were not given audience by Mehbooba. Instead, she would ask them to report to a defeated hawkish fellow, a mullah, Peerzada Mansoor and seek redressal. There were two Bhats in PDP, Nizamuddin Bhat and Abdul Rehman Bhat (Veeri), who are being humiliated by the party. In 2008, Mufti picked up a non-mullah from Tral assembly constituency and promised him mandate. The gentleman, a journalist, worked day and night and created space for himself in the constituency. When elections were close, an uneducated, unemployed mullah, Mushtaq Shah was picked and was given the ticket.

Caste & Class-driven Jihad

I sometimes feel obsessed with this *mullah factor*. Kashmiris know this is true of their land.

Mullahs are the ones spearheading the narrative of Azadi *ka matlab kya, La illaha illallah*. Common Kashmiri children are charged emotionally and readied for martyredom. The common Kashmiri is deliberately being pushed into the death-field. Mullahs are keeping common Kashmiris busy with bloodshed, while they capture the institutions and political power. *The common Kashmiri is being radicalised to get killed, so that the power corridors can forever remain the fiefdom of the mullahs.*

Who will make the sentimental common Kashmiri understand this game-plan? Why don't children of mullahs get radicalised? The fountainhead (the priest mullah) of radicalisation, Syed Ali Geelani too has children and grand children. They too have access to internet more than the average Kashmiri youth. Why is it that the entire generation of Kashmir's peasantry class has been, and continues to be radicalised online, and feels incited to kill 'them'?

I present a case study. I have two cousins, Taja and Mehmooda. Taja is married to a mullah and Mehmooda to a farmer. After marriage, both live in the same village where they grew up. In November 2017, I visited the Sher-e-Kashmir University of Agricultural Sciences and Technology. As I was walking toward the office of the Vice Chancellor, a young boy came running towards me. I could not recognise him. The boy told me he's the son of my cousin Taja. He had taken admission for a course at the university. In November 2018, my cousin Iftikhar sought my help in arranging hostel accommodation for Taja's other son, who had secured admission in M.Sc. Chemistry in Kashmir University. I felt happy for Taja.

Now let us see how Mehmooda fared. She has three daughters and a son. He was so highly radicalised that he left studies after Class XII to join militant ranks. It was very difficult for the family to stop him. Mehmooda had already suffered much in life. Her tears of total desperation and her threats that she would kill herself the moment he left finally stopped him. Two real sisters, two different stories.

Now let us study Shah Faesal, the Kashmiri who topped

the civil services examination in 2009. After a successful career as a bureaucrat, he recently announced his resignation from the civil services in early January, and floated his own political party. Shah Faesal's father was killed by militants, but his mother didn't surrender before destiny. She brought up her two sons with good education, and both became doctors. Shah Faesal later opted for the Civil Services and topped the examination.

Now let us visit Pulwama district in south Kashmir. Altaf Kachroo, a hard-core militant, was killed by security forces in an operation on 30 August 2018. Altaf was the son of Ghulam Muhammad Dar, who too was a militant. Dar was killed in the early '90s. Militant father, militant son.

Why is the non-mullah Kashmiri youth so radicalised? Why are children of mullah clans busy in securing good education and building their careers? This is a question that ordinary Kashmiri Muslims must ask themselves. Youth indoctrinated by radical Islam embrace death. They find life in death, while mullahs enjoy life.

Children of the Alchemist

This reminds me of what Farooq Maududi, son of Jamaat founder Maulana Maududi, stated in an interview to a Pakistani TV channel. The video is available on YouTube. Farooq said that the Maulana never allowed any of his nine children to even touch the literature he had written. Farooq stated in the interview that the Maulana would never keep his books in his house for the fear that his children would read them. On what was the reason for not allowing his children to study the books he had written or attend Jamaat congregations, Farooq said, 'Because he (Maulana Maududi) knew what poison was contained in that literature'.

The youth in Kashmir are under the sway of an ideology which seeks to reshape society and politics through the imposition of a radical understanding of Islam. But its preachers have kept this poisonous ideology out of their own homes. Instead, they have inculcated leadership skills among their children. Hence, we see the mullahs successfully debating on prime time or writing long and exhausting columns on 'subjugation and oppression'.

Mohammad Ashraf Sehrai, a non-mullah, replaced Syed Ali Geelani as the chairman of Tehreek-e-Hurriyat. Soon after Sehrai's ascent as chairman, his 28-year old son Junaid Ashraf Khan joined Hizbul Mujahideen. Did Sehrai have to pay this price for the ideology he represents? Or does he truly believe what he preaches, and had taken Islamism to his home?

In 2017, I asked senior separatist leader Professor AG Bhat, why he was sidelined. As usual, he started giving me a philosophical answer to my question. I told him he had been sidelined for two reasons. One, he didn't take diktats. And second, he was a non-mullah.

In the last week of December 2018, Mehbooba convened a meeting of her party leaders at her residence. Several leaders had deserted her, and many others were mulling options outside PDP. A senior leader told her that if she wanted to keep the flock together, she should show the door to her two lieutenants, Nayeem Akhtar Indrabi and Peerzada Mansur. Both are mullahs. Mehbooba outrightly rejected the proposal. She told the PDP members present that let everyone leave her party – she would prefer it over showing the door to her lieutenants.

The mullahs keep a close flock. This is how they rule over the emotionally vulnerable majority of non-mullah Kashmiri

Muslims. The mullahs sitting in the separatist camp enjoy power without responsibility. Some command mainstream politics. Others manage the affairs of the State as members of the State's powerful bureaucracy. Some control mind-space while sitting in television studios.

In 2016, violent street protests across the length and breadth of Kashmir had become the norm, and so the killings in retaliation. A dear friend of mine, Ghulam Muhammad Bhat of Khanyar, Srinagar asked his mullah friend, a separatist,'Why don't your children come out on streets?' The separatist's answer was shocking, 'Someone should be left to run the affairs of an independent Kashmir'.

His response captured the thinking of this class. The mullahs should be left to run the affairs of present-day Kashmir and be at the helm in post-independent Kashmir. Children of ordinary Kashmiris are expendable. They can continue to die for the utopia to be achieved.

I am concluding this chapter with the letter written by one Abdul Majid Banday, a Kashmiri settled in London. Banday wrote this letter to the Kashmiri leadership. It appeared on his facebook wall on 12 January 2019.

I wish Kashmiris here too start questioning separatist politics. Our youth must understand the dynamics of Kashmir politics and revisit the narratives propagated by the mullahs. The letter and the title given by Banday are reproduced below:

> **Ready To Join JRL (Joint Resistance Leadership viz Geelani, Mirwaiz, Malik), Albeit Have Some Reservations**
>
> Dear JRL, Asalamualikum to all of you.
>
> I am writing this letter to you being a common Kashmiri. Please don't look at it through the prism of an Indian

or a Pakistani narrative. The views and ideas expressed in this letter are totally my own. I am personally, solely responsible for the contents of this letter.

Everyone in J & K is the victim of circumstances. We have been the worst sufferers of conflict, chaos and ruthlessness of the prevailing order of the day. Every Kashmiri cutting across religious, ethnic or political lines has been the worst victim of bad times.

Recently I came across a news item, where you've asked Kashmiri youth to join resistance movement to strengthen it at grass-root level. Taking this news as a baseline, I thought to write to you.

Dear JRL, with high regards and respect for all of you, I, as a common Kashmiri may or may not agree with your political thought. However, this is equally true that you are the custodian of peoples' sentiments at large. You represent a constituency that touches the hearts of millions of Kashmiris. People pin their hopes on you for a peaceful and dignified resolution of Kashmir issue. There are more than hundred thousand Kashmiri people who sacrificed their lives for the resolution of Kashmir problem and an equal number of people either suffered brutal interrogations or were left devastated for the rest of their lives.

I am not in a position to dictate lessons of Kashmiri history to you. However, I do feel myself under moral obligation to put forth my narrative of freedom movement before you.

In my opinion, Kashmir issue has two dimensions – external & internal. Externally, this issue pertains to India & Pakistan, governed by UN resolutions. Internally, it works within the domain of India – Indian administered Kashmir & Pakistan – Pakistan Administered Kashmir. A dignified solution needs all three parties on the same page. How far have we progressed to bring all three parties on the same page? If we haven't, what is the future strategy in this regard?

As a common Kashmiri, I see people dying at a large-scale on daily basis. Hundreds and thousands of people have either disappeared or buried within unnamed graves. Widows, half-widows, orphans and destitute people constitute a large class of our ill-fated society. I am a witness to hundreds of deaths. Some of those killed were named as martyrs, while others were political workers or informers, who were not even given a proper religious funeral. We as common Kashmiris have a right to ask what you have done for those people who are living at the mercy of time? I know tens of people from Hurriyat camps who are unable to make their both ends meet. They have suffered tortures, harassment and became the social victims at times and are now living a miserable life. While some people in your camp raised to the level of leadership and are duly regarded as true representatives, thereby showered with luxuries of life, others were let down and left at the mercy of God.

I wonder if you have any program for those people who lost their everything for Kashmir cause? Their deplorable condition deters people like me to treat you as a viable political option.

We all know how we are suffering at the hands of occupation. Yes, we need a dignified resolution of our problems. But we are a population of fifteen million people having our day-to-day problems. What is the mechanism to address those issues? As leaders, you've been enjoying all facilities and even government security in certain cases. You are also given healthcare facilities and other perks, which we as a common people can't even dream of. Your kith and kin are appointed and absorbed in government but our merit is marred for no fault of our own.

Yes, your graph of sacrifices is too high. However, sadly, your sacrifices are directly proportional to your worldly gains. A million dollar question is: Unless India and Pakistan come together to find an everlasting solution to the Kashmir dispute, what in your opinion can a simple Kashmiri do in between this time? How can a population of millions of people address their day-to-day issues? What is the survival plan?

Strike and Chalo calls is good, but how does it help collective interests of a common Kashmiri? It may show your political strength or resentment of people towards occupation but its impact on economy, education and psychology on Kashmiri population is devastating. Most of the people treat these frequent shutdowns as a wake-up call for the international community which I, in my little capacity after spending several years abroad, believe is a total distortion of facts. International community is least bothered about Kashmir conflict and other related issues. For them, India is a big market and, unfortunately, they in no way can bear the brunt of this emerging economic global power. Thus, 'strike politics' has proved a worst blow on our overall economy.

Dear JRL, we know the state restrictions and bondings you are going through right from the eruption of armed struggle in Jammu and Kashmir. You are not even allowed to offer mandatory congregational prayers. You have been the worst sufferers of this turmoil being at the forefront. We don't expect you to resolve our developmental issues as you are not the part of an electoral politics. Given these facts, the only way by which we can judge your performance is how loyal you've been to the people who sacrificed everything for Kashmir!! Unfortunately, they are at the receiving end.

I have been in mainstream politics from the last more than a decade now. At times, I feel suffocated and humiliated but what is the other way around? I have no passion to contest elections but to serve myself and my people. If you can accommodate the likes of me, we are ready to move an extra mile.

There are many people like me who want to join your caravan, albeit we have some reservations & queries before we proceed further.

These include:

- Is Kashmir conflict a religious or political issue?
- When we speak about occupation, does it include Pakistan-administered Kashmir as well? What is our contribution on the other side of our J&K, commonly called as Azad J&K?
- We are unable to see any second line political leadership in any pro-freedom camp including JRL. I wonder if there is any?
- We are under brutal occupation. What is your plan to get rid of it?
- Unless we are set free by our occupiers, what is the survival plan?
- We want to know the progress of our struggle? How far have we achieved our target at national or international level during all these years of unprecedented struggle?

This list is not exhaustive.

Above all, with due regards to sentiments and aspirations, I, as a common Kashmiri am looking forward to an honest reply from all or anyone of you.

PS: Before my friends start bashing me, please read this letter between the lines and in its totality. Thank you all.

Kind Regards,

Abdul Maajid Banday
Handwara

Transformation of Kashmir's Society

THE LIBERAL leftists, sitting far from Kashmir, consider themselves sympathetic to the Kashmir cause. For all their good intentions, they cannot understand the churning that Kashmir's society is going through. Sympathisers in the outer world and apologists within Kashmir society look at the crises in Kashmir only through the prism of Indo-Pak conflict. They attribute everything happening in Kashmir to the failure of India and Pakistan in resolving this long-drawn dispute. The protagonists in Kashmir refuse to see the churning. They sell the narrative of 'political conflict' conveniently and successfully.

Kashmir sympathisers in mainland India keep stressing on resolution of the dispute to bring peace to this Himalayan region. They are honest in their viewpoint to the best of their understanding of the Kashmir crisis. Even the so-called stakeholders in Kashmir who are also apologists may be honest to a certain extent. But the problem has moved beyond the narrative of just a 'political conflict' in Kashmir. We need an honest ground analysis to suggest some measures which may defuse the situation.

An ideology seeks to reshape Kashmiri society through the imposition of a radical understanding of Islam. Islamists, particularly Jamaat-e-Islami in Kashmir, has increasingly resorted to both violence and political means to advance their cause of establishing Islamic rule in Kashmir. This happened long before Hindutva forces got prominence in the Indian mainstream. In 1987, Muslim United Front fought the election on the manifesto of establishing Sharia in Jammu and Kashmir. Whatever were the designs of Mufti Sayeed and Mir Qasim to bring Jamaat into mainstream politics in 1972, Jamaat jumped into the electoral process, promising to change the system from a secular democratic one to an Islamic one. Jamaat-e-Islami has categorically stated that it considers elections as a means to capture power and rewrite the constitution of Jammu and Kashmir. In that sense, the Jamaat and the RSS are first cousins.

The Jamaat's decision to participate in the elections in the past, as well as any decision regarding future participation does not mean that it has embraced Indian secularism and the Constitution. Yes, they are desperate in their desire to achieve power. The religious groups in Kashmir are in consonance with the Islamists in Pakistan and elsewhere, who are increasing their influence through strong mobilisation skills to establish the Sunni Islamic Caliphate, using both violent and non-violent tactics.

Jamaat was engaged in secret talks with New Delhi from 1999 to 2002 with two broad objectives. One was to secure the safety of its cadres from the onslaught of Indian security agencies and Kashmiri renegades. The other was to establish their legitimacy in all quarters where the Kashmir dispute was discussed. The Jamaat achieved both its objectives.

If the Jamaat agrees to contest any elections in the future, they will still secure the most favourable position for themselves. They may not win, but they will establish their claim of being the most legitimate stakeholders. The slogan of *Yehan kya chalega, Nizam-e-Mustafa* has to be seen in the right context. How has the Kashmiri society been impacted by the narratives of Islamism which originated from the conflict?

Two things are visible on the ground. One, the generation that emerged from the conflict guided by extremist narratives and in the shadow of the bullet has no respect for the value system. They have been brought up in a unique atmosphere where the syncretism and pluralism are considered as foreign impositions. They look at everything which may appear good and positive as a conspiracy. If you propagate the values of an inclusive, plural society, it is a conspiracy. The developmental evolution of the society is regarded as a conspiracy against them. There is outright rejection of whatever the government does with good intentions. Even if someone in his individual capacity intends to do something good for the society, he is looked upon with suspicion.

This is true not just about the youth. The malaise has spread across Kashmiri society. Every new initiative here is a conspiracy against Kashmir or Kashmiris. In March 2015, realising that prime-time news channels are spewing venom against Kashmiris, I proposed to my friends in the Kashmir civil society that we should bring some major names from the national media to Srinagar. Let them engage with their counterparts in Kashmir and assess the situation from ground zero. Senior journalists like Bashir Manzar, Tahir Mohiudin and Shujaat Bukhari helped me in my effort, and I started preparations.

Lehar organised the first media summit in SKICC Srinagar. Veteran journalists Kuldeep Nayyar, Sayeed Naqvi, Sidharath Vardarajan, Shahid Siddiqui, Madhu Kishwar, KG Suresh, Saba Naqvi, Rana Ayyub, Nidhi Kulpati, Rahul Jalali and other prominent journalists came at our invite to participate in the Srinagar Media Summit. A local journo spread the word in Press Colony, Srinagar, that it was a Government of India project. So, the entire Kashmir press, barring a few journalists, decided to boycott it. We had decided to honour cartoonist Bashir Ahmad Bashir, Ved Bhasin (posthumous), Sona Ullah Aftab (posthumous) and Balraj Puri (posthumous). Tahir Mohiudin, who was with us on the organising committee, didn't turn up. Bashir Ahmad Bashir switched off his phone and did not make it to the conference. Shujaat Bukhari was out of the country but had instructed his team to participate. Good that they turned up. I had literally begged the Tourism Department of Kashmir to sponsor the conference as it was genuinely a stakeholder.

In 2016, we organised the second edition of Kashmir's media summit. We organised it at Pahalgam this time. Again, journalists from various metropolitan cities participated in the conference, but not a single local journalist turned up for it. The reason was the same again. Some journalist had spread the word in the Press Colony that we were funded by Delhi. Our intention was to present Kashmir and Kashmiri people in the right perspective to the national media, and our effort made a difference. A freelance travel journalist who attended the conference wrote a detailed feature on it, presenting the 'real picture of Kashmir'. The feature was carried by scores of publications across the country. In the first half of 2018, we invited Sidharath Vardarajan, Rajdeep Sardesai, Shahid Siddiqui, Sagarika Ghosh, Suhasini Haider, Arfa Khanum, Santosh Bhartiya and many others to Kashmir, to interact with the youth. These eminent individuals greatly appreciated our efforts. But locally, the accusation remained the same. According to them, these were attempts to dilute the Kashmir dispute.

Traffic Rules are Subjugation

Islamisation of Kashmir and the Kashmir conflict has had a huge impact on the psychology of the young and furious generation of the Valley. Large sections of this generation have become bands of outlaws. There is no respect for law, and no realisation of responsibilities. Mahatma Gandhi had said, 'There are no rights except duties and from the duties well done follow the rights.' In Kashmir, particularly for the young generation, there are no duties and responsibilities towards society. Even adherence to traffic rules is seen as subjugation. In 2017, we organised a roundtable conference in Srinagar. A PhD scholar also participated in the conference. When it was his turn to speak, he started in rage and soon shouted, 'What kind of freedom are we enjoying here where a matriculate traffic policeman stops me at traffic light! How dare he?'

On social media in Kashmir, we keep seeing posts of the following kind. A policeman stops a motorcyclist. The motorcyclist removes his helmet and shouts, 'Hum kya chahte – Azadi!' in protest. If the government constructs roads, bridges or other physical infrastructure, the furious generation interprets these as an attempt at furthering 'Indian rule'. Thus, they believe that these physical assets must be demolished everytime the situation takes a violent turn. The talk of demolishing the symbols of pluralism and Sufism is normal in Kashmir. During street agitations demanding azadi, damage to private cars, ambulances, auto-rickshaws etc is common. If you resist this arrogance, you will be targeted.

There are hundreds of incidents where elderly people were dragged out of cars and beaten by youngsters in an act of rage, for daring to be out for some work during *hartal* calls. No one dared to intervene. No one condemned it.

Jungle Raj

Militants seem to be strategically emboldened in Kashmir after the withdrawal of US troops from Afghanistan. There are two emerging trends which can define the fate of Kashmir in the coming months. Withdrawal of US troops from Afghanistan has emboldened Islamists in the entire region. This will have a direct bearing on the situation in Kashmir. Terrorist infrastructure is flourishing in Pakistan and Afghanistan.

US, Afghanistan, Pakistan and India are likely to enter into a dialogue process with the Muslim militia groups in Afghanistan. What does this mean? The Islamic militia will get recognition on the table, whatever the outcome of the dialogue. This is what their political fountainheads like Jamaat-e-Islami are looking at. They know that recognition of the Islamic militia as a legitimate entity is a huge breakthrough, even if the dialogue fails. Jamaat and other extremist religious organisations are increasingly seeking to use the dialogue table as a means to implement their version of Islam on the Muslim countries.

Soon after the US announced its disengagement in Afghanistan, Hizbul's local commander Riyaz Naikoo sent out a video message. He urged the militant organisation in Pakistan to export militants to Kashmir to make it a decisive battleground. Naikoo has been outspoken in presenting the agenda of Islamisation of Kashmir. Lashkar-e-Taiba (LeT), Jaish-e-Muhammad (JeM) and other dreaded organisations have also clearly outlined their Mission Kashmir project. It is this influence and the combined strength of militant organisations in Pakistan which has made Syed Salahuddin identify himself with the global terror network.

Mission Kashmir

In Kashmir, it is evident from the pattern of encounters and the killing of militants that militant organisations active in Kashmir are cohesive both ideologically and physically. There is hardly any encounter where militants of two or three outfits are not trapped together in the same hideout. This was not the case before.

In the last week of December 2018, Zakir Musa's deputy was killed along with Hizbul militants in an encounter in Tral in south Kashmir. This indicates that all the militant groups are active in the same operational domain. Earlier, militant groups would not share the same physical domains, and would not share operational inputs with other groups. This is an indication that the conflict theatre of Kashmir has been influenced by the global jihad and all the militant groups operating in Kashmir are ideologically if not organisationally part of the global jihadism.

Going by the messages of Riyaz Naikoo[4] and Zakir Musa,

4 Riyaz Ahmad Naikoo also known as Mohammad bin Qasim (alias Zubair) was a militant commander in the pro-Pakistani Islamic-terrorist organisation Hizb-ul-Mujahideen. He was killed by Indian security frces on 6 May 2020

both are on the same page. The fight is no more for 'liberating' Kashmir. It has transformed into a pan-Islamic movement with both underground and overground operations. This transformation cannot be seen in isolation.

The cohesiveness in the terror ideology across the border has a direct impact on Kashmir. In 2015, an audio of Hizbul posterboy Burhan Wani and LeT chief Hafiz Sayeed vowing support to each other went viral in the Valley. This was a clear statement that henceforth, the affiliation or allegiance to a particular militant outfit would not matter.

All of them ideologically belong to one family. Since all of them derive their ideological and emotional force from jihad, their differences are no more relevant. Overground religious organisations in Kashmir too have buried their differences in their project of supporting jihad. Asking the Indian government to initiate dialogue in Kashmir has entirely different connotations now. It is about bringing overground Islamists to the talking table. The secularists have either been sidelined, or they too have adjusted with the changing narratives, as is the case with Yasin Malik of Liberation Front.

Any future dialogue initiative by the Government of India will bring to the table an entirely different perspective on Kashmir.

Islamisation has not only influenced Kashmir's society from within. It has equally changed the outlook of Kashmir's society vis-à-vis India. There is now the Hindu versus Muslim narrative. The narrative is that of 'Islam in danger'. The fast-growing Hindutva mindset has further helped the Islamists in consolidating this narrative. The mainstream political parties of Kashmir, including the National Conference (NC) and Peoples Democratic Party (PDP), have conditioned themselves to go along with the popular narrative. On ground, their cadres have mixed with religious groups. They are increasingly becoming apologists for Islamisation.

The same kind of posturing can be seen in Kashmir's civil society groups. There is hardly any window available for free flow of ideas. The mindspace in Kashmir is completely under the control of extremist ideology. The space for moderates or liberals has squeezed alarmingly. About six months before 2009 batch IAS topper Shah Faesal submitted his resignation, there were rumours that he would join Omar Abdullah's National Conference. Kashmir was anticipating his resignation and his joining the NC simultaneously. But the intensity of abuses being hurled at him was so severe that he was pushed to the backfoot and deferred his decision. It is not just that social media tigers dominate the discourse in Kashmir. This is a true reflection of the ground situation. The furious generation has an irrational approach to everything, including their own lives. Their approach is now ruling the roost.

Rationalism and logic have died with the death of pluralism in Kashmir. The generation of conflict is far more aggressive, irrational and insane than Shah Faesal would have ever anticipated. This actually marks a shift in the collective thinking of the Kashmir society – a society which is demographically young now.

The reasons to fight the state have changed. So have the dimensions of the problem. The rise of Hindutva forces in mainland India and the insecurity among minorities has strengthened the cause of Islamists in Kashmir. The attacks on minorities after the 2014 election have changed the thinking of people in Kashmir who were earlier considered moderates. Extremists feed each other. Islamists find it easier than ever before to instigate and indoctrinate young minds. The desire to change the status quo is increasing.

Tackling extremism in Kashmir is now more difficult–given the kind of narratives popular in the mainland. It is very important to understand the genesis of the problem. Only then one can suggest remedial measures. It is established globally that violent extremism, popularly known as terrorism, has to be dealt with, with a combination of coercive and conciliatory policies. It is imperative that these policies do not undermine each other by being used against the wrong audiences. Voices of reason from the Indian mainland have been insisting that coercive measures should be restricted to militants. Their potential recruits should be approached with reconciliatory measures. In the present Kashmir context, there is also need for a third strategy.

The Government of India will find it difficult to normalise the situation in Kashmir by security and political responses alone. Security measures are essential to tackle militancy in order to deactivate the violent groups. There is no reason for them to talk if they are at a position of bargaining. Political measures are equally important to restore the hope of the civilian majority. The Government of India has wasted much time in responding politically to the situation in Kashmir. But *there is always an option, immaterial of how terribly the narratives on ground have changed from seeking basic human rights to visualising an Islamic state.*

Top generals of the Indian Army have successively admitted in media interviews that security measures are not enough to resolve the situation. Depending on these alone to achieve the desired results would be disastrous. The government has also realised in Kashmir that if you kill one, you are leading to two recruitments in militancy.

Political response to the conflict is essential for two reasons. One, Kashmir was essentially considered a political problem at the beginning by all stakeholders but shifted the narrative. To reinvent the political issue, you need to talk politics. Two, engagement brings hope on the table.

'Doing something nice without really doing it' is the first requirement of political engagement. Here is an example of how the Kashmir psyche works. In September 2016, when Kashmir was still burning in the aftermath of the Burhan Wani episode, a group of senior journalists visited Kashmir on my request. Prem Shankar Jha, who was part of the delegation, insisted that I must arrange a meeting of the group with some separatists. I managed contact with a couple of them. We went to meet them at their respective residences, because they were under house arrest. One separatist leader, while expressing his anguish over non-engagement said, 'Earlier they (people in Delhi) would greet us on the occasions of Eid. Even that is not happening now'. Non-engagement can play an instrumental role in transforming the conflict from political to militant.

President Kennedy said, 'A willingness to resist force, unaccompanied by a willingness to talk, could provoke belligerence – while a willingness to talk unaccompanied by a willingness to resist could invite disaster'. Leading strategist on conflict resolution, I William Zartman has said – for dealing with terrorism, it is essential to keep violent means in check, transform its end from destruction to participation, and undercutting the grievances on which it rides. RAND Corporation study of 2008, 'How Terrorist Groups End' by Seth G Jones and Martin C Libicki, 2008, looked at 648 terrorist groups since 1968. The study concluded that 43%

terrorist groups ended in transition to a political process, 40% ended as a result of policing, 10% ended with victory for the terrorists, and only 7% ended as a result of military success.

Despite the risks involved in negotiating with violent extremists, the risks of adopting a non-negotiation policy are more deadly. It is essential for the state to enter into a process of dialogue at the appropriate time. Unfortunately, where Kashmir is concerned, India has wasted many appropriate opportunities. Equally, the Kashmir separatist camp has missed the bus at least on four occasions in the last 30 years. The lost opportunities on both sides will be discussed in a separate chapter.

Now for the third strategy that I spoke about. The Kashmir conflict has witnessed a dangerous transformation. It is essential for the Government of India to go beyond security and political measures. Emergence of rightwing politics on the political landscape in the Indian mainland and assertion of Hindutva forces has impacted the overall Kashmir situation. It has also drawn a Lakshman Rekha.

The long-forgotten Gujral doctrine, Left parties succeeding in incorporating 'autonomy' in the Common Minimum Programme of the HD Deve Gowda government, PV Narsimha Rao's 'sky is the limit' statement, Vajpayee's, '*Insaniyat ke dayre mein*' – all these developments and catchy phrases have lost relevance with the advent of Hindutva forces on the political landscape of India.

Rahul Gandhi is fighting the BJP brand of Hindutva with his version of soft Hindutva. Ghulam Nabi Azad, Salman Khursheed and other Muslim leaders of the Congress are hardly ever seen campaigning in Hindu-majority areas. One cannot expect any 'out of the box' thinking from them regarding Kashmir.

During his visit to Kashmir in 2016, Mani Shankar

Aiyar told a gathering, 'How stupid you people are! Such an unprecedented agitation, but at what time? When Modi – the RSS man – is ruling the country. You should have deferred it till 2019 or even to 2024 when someone like Manmohan Singh would be sitting in Delhi, who could feel the pain and urgency of reaching out to you'.

The Third Eye

I have often reiterated in conferences on Kashmir – within Kashmir and in mainland India – about major perceptional problems. Kashmiris are entrenched in history. They are still trapped in 1947 and the vital dates thereafter. The Government of India, on the other hand, is not ready even to go back to April 2004, when Atal Bihari Vajpayee invoked the '*Insaniyat ke dayre mein*' strategy.

We Kashmiris have been conditioned to stay hooked to history – that too selectively. People in mainland India do not look towards history. They are futuristic. The third strategy to improve the situation in Kashmir is the propagation of 'truth'. Not the jihadi 'truth' but the 'truth' in its unblemished avatar.

Kashmir is landlocked mentally and physically. If you want to bring peace to Kashmir, you have to connect it to the external world (not the Muslim world). You need to build fresh narratives based on rational and scientific temperament. This is where the Government of India has failed miserably. Bring the world to Kashmir, if you cannot take Kashmir to the world. Also, resolution of the Kashmir conflict must not be linked to electoral processes.

Elections are a regular feature in mainland India. But India cannot afford to look at Kashmir through the narrow prism of electoral politics. India must be consistent in its

Kashmir policy, irrespective of who forms the government in Delhi. Despite the dangerous transformation that Kashmir has witnessed during recent years, one hope is still alive. The ambitious and aspirational instinct of the Kashmiri youth. We need to build on it and expose the Kashmiri youth to the outside world. The homogeneity of Kashmir has blocked the youth's mindspace. Veteran journalist Sayeed Naqvi had visited Kashmir when Lehar organised the Srinagar Media Summit in 2015. He recounted to us something his brother said after visiting Pakistan: 'A lively place but too many Muslims around.'

This is not limited to Muslims alone. The exclusive presence of any religious group in a particular area can be unhealthy. The social fabric of Kashmiri society was damaged by the exodus of Kashmiri Pandits. Deep penetration of the radical interpretations of Islam destroyed Kashmir's social fabric. It is essential to expose the Kashmiri youth to multi-cultural and inclusive societies to make them realise the essence of such societies.

What should be the modus operandi of such an initiative?

I have consistently maintained that the Instrument of Accession is an agreement between the people of Jammu and Kashmir, and the people of India. It is an agreement between 120 crores of Indians and 1 crore Kashmiris. No stakeholder can undo it unilaterally. The people of the Union of India form the biggest category of stakeholders in the Kashmir conflict. It is the responsibility of the larger Indian civil society to help in bringing peace in Kashmir. India cannot afford to leave the conflict to the various governments for resolution. Governments in democracies like India are more for the conflict, than for its resolution. The Indian civil society has a very major role in Kashmir, which unfortunately it has failed to realise.

Only the Indian civil society can help in rationalising the

narratives in Kashmir. It must convince the government to look at the issue through the human prism. I once decided to take a group of Indian women achievers to Kashmir. My objective was that women in rural Kashmir must interact with these achievers from mainland India, and see that these confident, dynamic women also live on the same planet. I tried several times to bring achievers like renowned author, writer, journalist and feminist Shobhaa De or tennis star Sania Mirza to Kashmir. Once they interact with Kashmir's women, they will influence the intellectual discourse here. Second, I wanted them to interact with as many women as possible, in order to demolish the mental barriers of rural women. There is urgent need for coordinated civil society initiatives to rationalise the deadly narratives in Kashmir.

Lost Opportunities: Redefining Delhi-Srinagar Relations

I ONCE asked former RAW chief AS Dulat about the 'Dulat doctrine' that people keep talking about. What is it precisely? 'Talking', he said. It's about 'Talking'. 'Keep talking.' Talking about what? was my next question. He said 'Talking' is not the same as 'Negotiating'.

There are a number of steps before negotiation begins.

How have conflicts across the world been negotiated? What are the basic requirements for sitting across the table to sort out issues? FW de Klerk identifies three stages to South African negotiations from the government's viewpoint. First, an exploratory phase with Nelson Mandela and the ANC in exile. Second, informal talks to remove obstacles and prepare for structured negotiations. Third, formal and representative negotiations that led to a new constitution in South Africa.

Niel Barnard identifies six phases of negotiation. Establishing contact and information gathering; building trust; exploring the range of opportunities; transferring the process to a wider base; the return of exiles; formal negotiations which can lead to a settlement.

During a dialogue with PLO in Palestine, four phases were identified by the government negotiators. Fact finding; authorisation for the talks; legitimisation of the channel; breakthrough from the back channel to the official talks.

How have rebel groups across the globe reached the dialogue table? Rebels identified three stages for the peace process to the EI Salvador conflict. One, using political negotiations as a device to support war. Two, using war to support negotiations. Finally, negotiations which are central to rule out war.

Whatever the conflict and whosoever the stakeholders – whatever its nature, tractable or intractable, there are distinct stages involved in its resolution. These are establishing contact, building communication channels, restoring confidence and building trust, understanding and recognising each other's limitations.

The first contact is always established on behalf of the government by its intelligence agencies. They are trained for the purpose, and also for the ability to act deniably. The British government had a secret channel to communicate with the Irish Republican Army (IRA). The contact was established as early as in 1972 – 22 years before the bloodshed finally ended.

There are always testing times in the process. Intelligence agencies are conditioned to move forward despite all hiccups. Intelligence agencies establish contact with rebels to act as mediators and facilitate negotiations on behalf of the government. They are skilled to the level that they appear to be neutral.

Negotiating Peace in Kashmir

Keeping in mind these defined roadmaps for negotiations, let us examine whether there were any opportunities to break the deadlock between the separatists and the Indian government?

Had the Kashmiris comprehended the different stages involved in conflict resolution?

Or did they take to armed rebellion with no idea of its consequences? The fact is that Kashmiris had no idea of the fallout of a violent militancy. The youth took to it, as if undertaking an adventure. Some disgruntled youngsters went across the border, came back with AK 47s in their hands. Innocent Kashmiris kissed the barrels of their guns with faith and hope, as if 'freedom' was around the corner.

In the jointly authored *The Spy Chronicles,* AS Dulat tells us, 'When Kashmir's turmoil started, I was posted in Srinagar. Kashmiri boys were going (to Pakistan) and coming, and we asked locals what was happening. They said crossing the border was normal, no big deal. It started with a handful of guys, five JKLF boys. One thing led to another. Unfortunately, in December 1989, Mufti Saheb's daughter's kidnapping became a watershed in Kashmir. It gave the boys confidence that they could get the Government of India to give in to their demands. Kashmiris started believing they might get azadi. They turned their watches back half an hour'. Even Pakistan had not realised how far this transaction would and could go.

The former ISI chief Asad Durrani concedes in *The Spy Chronicles* that Pakistan had expected that the insurgency would not last for more than six months. 'When the uprising began, we were just marking time to see what happens', Durrani said. Pakistan steadily got more involved, leading to the rise of Hizbul Mujahideen.

ISI tried to weaponise JKLF as early as in 1984, but its Valley-based cadres refused to do so.

It was only after Amanullah Khan came back to Pakistan after self-exile in 1986 that the decision to arm JKLF cadres was taken. One of the turning points in contemporary Kashmir history was 1989. The common Kashmiris gullibly accorded social sanction to gun culture, and they started identifying with the violent narrative.

Pakistan was finally convinced that the time had now come when new extremist groups could replace JKLF. The Jamaat-e-Islami was set up and ISI put its weight behind Jamaat-e-Islami. The Jamaat gained ascendency despite the fact that it had a very limited appeal till then in Kashmir. Since Huzbul Mujahideen was established as the armed wing of Jamaat, it suited Pakistan ideologically to replace JKLF with Hizbul.

However, ISI didn't rely on Hizbul alone. It created several armed groups. Soon Kashmir witnessed massive killings in group clashes. Hizbul carders and its overground ideologues of Jamaat-e-Islami went on the rampage to eliminate the 'other', the militants affiliated to other groups, people having different political and ideological affiliations, the political workers. Hundreds were eliminated in group clashes. Militants affiliated with other groups such as JKLF, Students Liberation Front, Al-jihad, Ikhawanul Muslimeen, Al-baraq were massacred in large numbers.

Violence has phases. It expands with the expansion of military means. When Pakistan felt that its control over the Kashmir conflict was weakening, it formed the Hurriyat Conference to sublet the contract of conflict. Hurriyat Conference was created as a political platform by Pakistan to visualise, assess and analyse how they could bargain with the

Government of India. It was, however, just a conglomeration of power-hungry brokers, not negotiators.

Study conflicts across the globe and consider how they were resolved. You will find that of all the factors contributing to the possibility of a successful negotiation, political leadership plays the most crucial role. *If the two sides have a pro-active leadership prepared to take risks, settlement is more likely.*

Hurriyat Conference is an amalgam of individuals who sorely lacked the leadership that Kashmir needed. The Kashmir conflict has thrown up challenges and also opportunities. Hurriyat Conference has consistently failed in realising these opportunities to steer Kashmir in the right direction. If they had done so, Kashmir would not have been the mess it is today.

With passage of time, Pakistan developed huge interest in keeping the pot boiling. This was the real test for the Kashmiri separatists. Did they care for Kashmir, or were they simply representing Pakistan's interest in Kashmir?

Whether it was because of the violent militancy, at the behest of the US or other international players, the Indian government expressed willingness many times to negotiate with the separatists in order to redefine the Centre-State relationship. Unfortunately, the separatists, particularly Syed Ali Geelani of Jamaat-e-Islami, sabotaged these efforts every time. The many many opportunities were wasted.

Geelani has been caught in the snare of preconditions for two reasons. One, Geelani lacks a solid argument. He has never been a good negotiator. He is like a robot conditioned for certain actions. On many occasions, he has appeared on national news channels. Every time, he has left without responding to the legitimate questions. More than often he leaves without listening to a contrary viewpoint.

He never agrees to share the stage with those who don't subscribe to his views. Even if he agrees, he sets the pre-condition that he will speak and leave. This is his personal makeup. He cannot debate and discuss. This reminds me of Mufti Sayeed's style. He would speak less, but he was not a good listener either. He would rarely listen.

His close aide once asked me why Mufti spoke seldom and so little. I replied that he is not a good speaker. He agreed to what I said. Likewise, Geelani is a disaster as far as arguing goes. He represents Pakistan's deep state more than he claims to represent Kashmir. He does not move an inch unless asked to do so. His refusal to be part of any negotiating table since the 1990 has cost Kashmir and Kashmiris dear.

What happened to the negotiations that other Hurriyat leaders were part of?

Government of India's follies and faults apart, the Hurriyat leaders who were ever on the negotiating table with India have faced a real threat to their lives, and have hence vacillated in their response. *The threat they faced was from Geelani.* Kashmir has seen many eminent individuals who had disagreements with Geelani. They were all killed. Abdul Gani Lone, Mirwaiz Farooq, Qazi Nisar Ahmad, Ghulam Qadir Wani are a few to name.

Politics and the Parties

Militancy was still in its infancy in 1989-90, when VP Singh's government was at the helm. The government failed to realise the importance of dialogue. Those familiar with Kashmir politics could see the reason. Mufti was the second most-important man in that government. Farooq Abdullah was the chief minister in Jammu and Kashmir.

Mufti's personal animosity superseded national interest. He was not in favour of giving concessions to Farooq. Rather, Mufti wanted Farooq's unceremonious exit. Mufti succeeded in achieving this after he appointed Jagmohan as Governor of Jammu and Kashmir for his second inning.

From 1991 to 1996, two important developments took place. In 1995, Prime Minister PV Narsimha Rao made a fervent appeal from Burkina Faso in Africa, saying that 'sky is the limit' for the quantum of autonomy to the State of Jammu and Kashmir, within the Constitution of India.

This was an appeal for the mainstream parties, particularly National Conference, to start the democratic process in Kashmir. The democratic process had been paralysed after the inception of militancy, followed by the resignation of Chief Minister Farooq Abdullah. People generally accuse Farooq of not pursuing the PM's commitment for restoration of autonomy. It is partly true. After coming to power in 1996, Farooq Abdullah should have pressed for securing autonomy for the State.

But we are ignoring one thing. Why would the Indian government offer any concession to Farooq Abdullah, Mehbooba or some other mainstream leader if the separatists did not vow to end separatism? The question here was of dousing the flames. If those who put the house on fire were still holding combustibles, why would the Government of India offer anything to someone who was sitting inside the house and was part of the mainstream?

Although constantly pitting for dialogue with the separatists, mainstream politicians in Kashmir have steadily surrendered space to the separatist camp and accorded legitimacy to them.

They essentially played it for votes, but they went terribly wrong. This gross error cost them the legitimacy they would have enjoyed as mainstream political forces in Kashmir. By vouching for the representation of Hurriyat on the table, they put a big question mark to their own representative character. The strategic move should have been that the mainstream parties should have themselves sought a dialogue with the armed groups. Then their representative character would not have been dented.

It is the mainstream in Kashmir that has painted a larger-than-life picture of the separatists. No political player in Kashmir vested its energies into obtaining a clear insight of an armed conflict, and how it changes the political landscape in the conflict-ridden region. Had they vouched for a direct dialogue with the armed rebels, their own space would not have got squeezed. They would have led the peace talks and such peace talks would not be hostage to separatists.

Narasimha Rao lost the election during the same time when Farooq took over in 1996. But the promise had been made by the Prime Minister of India, and not Mr Rao in his personal capacity. Separatists should have responded to his promise. They would have achieved something even after Narsimha Rao's ouster. This became a lost opportunity.

After Rao, a coalition government led by HD Deve Gowda succeeded the Congress in Delhi. Supported by Left parties, Deve Gowda incorporated 'autonomy to Jammu and Kashmir' in his support group's common minimum programme. This was for the first time that any government at the Centre had committed itself to the restoration of autonomy to Jammu and Kashmir documentarily. The separatists again failed to respond.

The local communist leader, Yusuf Tarigami, who had enjoyed much confidence of veteran Marxist Harkishan Singh Surjeet, the then Secretary General of CPI(M), played a pivotal role in incorporating the greater autonomy concept in this Common Minimum Programme. The separatists again failed to respond.

Separatists in Kashmir follow a unique unconventional and irrational pattern. They fail to respond because they do not want to respond. This may be because they are not an independent entity. They speak for Pakistan, and not for Kashmir. And neither Pakistan nor separatists, want autonomy for Kashmir.

In conflicts, if you are speaking from the position of strength, you can impose conditions and riders for entering into negotiation. It is foolish to impose riders when you don't have bargaining power.

Kashmiri separatists, particularly Geelani, repeatedly take up the same position/stand and refuse to read the ground situation. In 2000, some seriousness was exhibited by the Government of India in resolving the conflict both internally and externally. Hizbul Mujahideen declared ceasefire on 24 July 2000, for unconditional talks with the Government of India. Hizbul chief Abdul Majid Dar took the initiative for talks. Initially it seemed as if the ISI, along with Hizbul supremo Muhammad Yusuf Shah, had approved the plan because Majid Dar came from Pakistan for talks.

This gave some hope to Kashmiris, who had been bearing the brunt of the bloody and armed confrontation. Their hopes were belied after Dar ended the ceasefire on 8 August 2000, under pressure from across the border.

Rhetoric of All or Nothing

All militant groups active in Kashmir are operating from Pakistan. Therefore, they negotiate primarily for Pakistan's interests. Hence talking to militant groups in Kashmir has its drawbacks. But in order to end the conflict, one has to *talk* to the rebels. The state cannot eliminate all the rebels, neither can the state change the militant mindset unless it talks to them directly.

Diplomatically and strategically, it is possible to understand and influence their viewpoint. Perhaps Majid Dar failed to realise that he had to negotiate on behalf of Pakistan, and not as a representative of Kashmiris. The dialogue thus collapsed. The Pak-supported Hurriyat consistently opposed the dialogue between the Hizbul and New Delhi, and sabotaged the process till it collapsed.

In 2004, another dialogue process started between Hurriyat – without Geelani – and the Government of India. On the India-Pakistan front too there was some forward momentum. Since Geelani was not part of the dialogue, it remained elusive. Those who were part of the dialogue process were skeptical about Geelani's sabotage politics, and other factors were at play too.

Geelani is a good hawk. He can sabotage a process, but you cannot make him sit at the table and argue. In *The Spy Chronicles*, former ISI chief Asad Durrani referred to the 2000 peace package of the prime minister of Israel Ehud Barak. Durrani said what Ehud Barak offered to Yasser Arafat looked good on surface. 'If you looked deeply, you might have found weaknesses. But it had that wisdom, that spirit', said Durrani.

Durrani stated further that may be the Prophet's accepting the Treaty of Hudaybiyyah 'was intended to teach us all the need to compromise and the criticality of timing. When the Palestinians objected to various provisions in the package, it was as if they could only compromise if Israel agreed to all concessions. It was a mistake. The summit failed'.

The former ISI chief then offered some valuable words of advice. 'Take whatever you can. You never have to say it is over.' *Durrani said the thing to do was to take what was on offer, improve one's position, and come back after a decent interval to ask for more.*

Geelani never displayed this wisdom or farsightedness. In *The Spy Chronicles*, Dulat reveals that before Sheikh Abdullah went ahead with the Afzal Beg (Parthasarthy) accord in 1975, he sent Farooq Abdullah to Pakistan. Farooq was told by Zulfiquar Ali Bhutto that 'they (Pakistan) were not in a position to help you, take what you can get. If you are offered peace and power in Kashmir, take it.'

Dulat also reveals that Yasin Malik was advised by Americans to do business with Delhi. When Yasin said that Delhi was unreasonable, they had said: You should take what you can get. 'They said it was not the final arrangement, but if something is on offer, grab it'.

There are moments in your journey where you have to leave the rhetoric of everything or nothing. When we want all or nothing, we may end up in getting nothing. 'Take what you can get' is the best approach in moving towards the final resolution. This light has not dawned upon separatists in Kashmir. They missed the bus at least five times during the last three decades.

The Orgy of Violence

Who should be held accountable for the continuing bloodshed in Kashmir?

The mainstream pays the price for mishandling the situation, whichever party is in power. We held Omar accountable in 2010 and voted him out. We held Mehbooba responsible in 2016 and she is discredited. What about Geelani and other separatists who failed on many occasions, and the Kashmiris continue to pay heavily for their mistakes? An emotionally charged and exploited population cannot afford to ignore the blunders committed by Geelani and others for long. This refusal to look at Geelani's misdeeds has resulted in anarchy in Kashmir. *Those claiming to be fighting for the rights of the people are actually snatching the people's right to life.* And Kashmir today refuses to acknowledge this.

A police contingent guards the grave of Sheikh Muhammad Abdullah for security reasons. He could not be held responsible for all that happened in Kashmir during his time. Conspiracies were hatched against him. He was a victim of those conspiracies. If Kashmiris someday realise who has turned their heaven into hell, a company of J&K Armed Police will have to guard Geelani's grave.

Suitable opportunities were wasted by the Indian state too. It is to be blamed for its share of not responding to the situation at the right time. *The Government of India failed to convince Kashmiris with genuine gestures that could act as a breakthrough towards bringing peace to the region.*

From 2002 to 2007, there was a sharp decline in violence in Kashmir. This was the right time to make some appropriate gestures. The Manmohan Singh-led UPA government showed some seriousness in reaching out to the people of Jammu and Kashmir. Unfortunately, nothing came of it due to disagreement within the Congress party.

In 2005, the separatists were told by Pakistan President Pervez Musharraf that there was immense pressure on him from the US to stop cross-border terrorism, so they should look at some other options of keeping the pot boiling. It was Musharraf who gave them the idea of stone-pelting to keep the violent phase going. He called it *intifada*, inspired perhaps by the Palestinian context with which the word is particularly associated.

This was also a time when General Pervez Musharraf categorically conveyed to Kashmiri separatists to engage with New Delhi, even if it meant participation in the electoral process to prove their representative character. However, ISI was not interested in the engagement of separatists with New Delhi, resulting in breakdown of the communication channels between separatists and New Delhi.

But this also remains an established fact that New Delhi too was not serious in taking on board the separatists. Had Delhi seized this opportunity, it would have changed the ground situation to a large extent. Dialogue between the parties, however, remains elusive – rather – has no significance when the nature of the conflict changes from a political to a religious, rather – a communal one. The Islamists of Kashmir with the overt and covert support of Pakistan deep state shifted the goal post by bringing in Islam into the conflict.

With the advent of Maududi form of Islam from Pakistan to Kashmir, we are now facing a situation where talking to separatists has little or no significance. The narrative is now Islamic in its contours. The Hurriyat's legitimacy over representing the sentiments of Kashmiris has suffered a huge blow. Their politics was nurtured on the political nature of the conflict. Now when religion is the narrative, Hurriyat has become irrelevant. This realisation has dawned upon the entire separatist camp, including Yasin Malik of JKLF. They are forced to identify themselves with the new narrative. Only Geelani, a survivor, continues to remain in the power play.

Now, Jamaat and some other religious groups have monopoly over the fresh narrative. Kashmir has surrendered its uniqueness to the new narrative of politicised Islam. *The desire to recover social capital and to restore the traditional society based on principles of coexistence and common syncretic identity does not have even peripheral significance.*

Exodus of Kashmiri Pandits

THE UNFORTUNATE exodus of Kashmiri Pandits in the 1990s had a major impact on how Kashmir's contemporary identity was defined and shaped. The exodus subjected the entire community to the worst kind of human tragedy possible – destitution and migration. It also changed forever the demography and political identity of Kashmir Valley.

In its fight against the autocratic Maharaja's rule, Kashmir had asserted a political identity which transcended narrow religious limitations. This identity was shaped by Kashmir's secular cultural ethos, which had laid the foundations for an inclusive, pluralistic democratic society.

Even though the Muslim identity was politicised first, it did not define the politics of Kashmir. The leadership at that time decided consciously to strengthen the social fabric by asserting the politically inclusive secular identity. This was resisted by mullahs in Kashmir and Panjabi Muslims in the Jammu region. In the beginning, they did not succeed in diluting this inclusiveness of Kashmir politics.

When militancy erupted in 1990, it dealt a blow to this inclusive character. The question which pits Kashmiri Pandits against Kashmiri Muslims is this: Who was responsible for the mass exodus of an entire community which seems to have lost its home and hearth forever? Kashmiri Pandits blame Kashmiri Muslims, particularly militants.

The Jagmohan Factor

On the other hand, the popular narrative among Kashmiri Muslims about the exodus is that Governor Jagmohan threw them out under a sinister plan to bulldoze Kashmiri Muslims. Kashmir's politicians, particularly the ruling class, could have connected the dots regarding the exodus. They conveniently remained silent on the issue at critical times. They speak about it occasionally now, but not in context. The politicians too held Jagmohan responsible for this act, whenever they spoke from political platforms.

Kashmiri Pandits have consistently rejected the theory that there were government plans behind their exodus. They insist that they were forced to leave by the militants and their overground supporters. Sometimes, the debate over the exodus becomes so murky that it overshadows the conflict. The question of who benefitted from the exodus sometimes takes centre stage.

Reservation for Kashmiri Pandits in government jobs, reservation for their children in educational institutions across the country, monetary relief, salaries and other benefits – these figure in the debates both in and out of Kashmir on the issue. Kashmiri Pandits speak of what they went through, and how difficult their life was. The debate over exodus is highly polarised and political, bereft of the human angle.

Even the literature that has been written since 1990 by writers from both communities is often prejudiced, biased and communal. It never speaks of the tragedies and sufferings of the other community. Post militancy, Kashmir produced a host of writers from both communities. They confined themselves to their respective communities. *They do not speak about how the collective conscience of the Kashmir society was hurt by violence beyond redemption.*

There is a trend among Kashmiri Muslim writers. Each one takes an orphan to the grave of his father killed by Indian security forces, and makes the child cry. The orphan is stimulated to stay at the grave of his father to forever cry, wail and mourn. He is not inspired to leave the tragedy behind and move forward in life.

Writers compete in making people cry and mourn. The same pattern is followed by most Kashmiri Pandit writers. *The invisible hands behind the exodus are debated more than the return of the Pandits to Kashmir.*

It was a stroke of fate that during this critical period of Kashmir history, Mufti Mohammad Sayeed was India's Home Minister. He served in this capacity from December 1989 to November 1990. At that time, Farooq Abdullah was the chief minister of Kashmir. He was also Mufti's chief political rival.

In order to weaken Farooq politically, Mufti Mohammad Sayeed influenced Prime Minister VP Singh to appoint Jagmohan as the Governor of the State. This was petty politics at its best. The same Jagmohan had dismissed Farooq Abdullah's government in July 1984, in his previous stint as Governor. Farooq was not on good terms with Jagmohan.

The Rajiv-Farooq accord of 1986 had a significant political impact on Kashmir.

GM Shah's government was dismissed on 12 March 1986 by Jagmohan during his first stint as the Governor of Jammu and Kashmir. During his time as chief minister, GM Shah had sparked communal passion in Jammu by building a mosque close to a temple in the Civil Secretariat premises. Shah's government was dismissed following communal riots in south Kashmir.

Farooq was made caretaker chief minister to supervise the elections scheduled for the next year. The accord didn't auger well with Mufti, who at that time was Tourism Minister in Rajiv's government. Mufti was waiting for an appropriate opportunity to sabotage the accord. The Meerut riots of 1986 (Hindu-Muslim conflict) provided him that opportunity.

Mufti resigned from the union cabinet in what he termed as his protest against the mishandling of the Meerut riots by the government. Back in Kashmir after his resignation, Mufti addressed a public rally at the sports stadium in Anantnag. There, he invoked Islam and said that he stood for the safety and security of Muslims.

From Mufti's perspective, the Rajiv-Farooq accord meant another six-year term for Farooq Abdullah as chief minister of Jammu and Kashmir. Mufti had been making overt and covert efforts since long to see himself in the chief minister's chair. Now the CM's office seemed a distant dream again.

Mufti had also realised that the Congress in Kashmir Valley was not strong as far as the number game was concerned. Staying in the Congress, Mufti wanted to change the discourse in Kashmir from secular (represented by Sheikh Abdullah and later his son) to religious. This is why he had convinced Jamaat-e-Islami in 1972 to contest the elections. Mufti's calculation was that though Sheikh was a secularist, he was equally popular on the religious platform. Mufti's objective was to somehow dilute Sheikh's monopoly over the religious platform (which was till then the traditional Sufi form of Islam) and create space for himself through introducing Maududi Islam.

After addressing the public rally at Anantnag, Mufti went to his hometown, Bijbehara, to mobilise his workers for some cynical plan. At that time, Jammu was already tense over the construction of a mosque near a temple. With Mufti's tacit approval, some temples and other Pandit properties were set ablaze in Bijbehara, Anantnag and Shopian in south Kashmir, and Sopore (hotbed of Jamaat-e-Islami) in the north.

I remember, after the destruction of temples in south Kashmir, Mufti visited many affected areas. At Akora village in his home constituency, Mufti was slapped by a Kashmiri Pandit Advocate, Pran Nath. Pran Nath, while accompanying Mufti to the temple site, had told him that the temple was totally damaged. Mufti, in a very irresponsible manner, had responded, 'Koi nahi, ek aur patthar rakh lo wahan par'. On this, Pran Nath slapped his face in protest.

The State went into elections in 1987 and Farooq Abdullah made a comeback. The elections, however, are considered the most controversial ever in Jammu and Kashmir and put a question mark on the authenticity of the results. And come 1989, the Valley was in the middle of a violent uprising. I am trying to understand the exodus of Kashmiri Pandits from two angles to put things in context. Was there any link between the vandalisations of properties of Kashmiri Pandits in 1986 in some selective areas of Kashmir and the exodus of 1990?

Come 1989, the Valley was in the middle of a violent uprising.

Mufti knew that the appointment of Jagmohan as Governor would irritate Farooq and make him quit. Farooq had earlier publicly stated that he would quit as chief minister if Jagmohan was made the Governor. But the Central Government went ahead bullishly shortsighted and made Jagmohan again the Governor of Jammu and Kashmir on the night of 19 January 1990. Farooq resigned the next day.

We must, therefore, try to understand the exodus of Kashmiri Pandits from two angles to put things in context. One: Was there any link between the vandalisation of temples in 1986 in some select areas of Kashmir, and the exodus of 1990? Was the agenda of exodus set in 1986? Or did the exodus happen with the inception of militancy?

It is known in Kashmir that Mufti engineered the 1986 vandalisation of Pandit properties. Come 1990, he was the Home Minister of India. Mufti is the only common link between 1986 and 1990. It may have been a mere coincidence. But it may not be a strange coincidence. This remains a subject of investigation.

Let us consider the opposing narratives of Kashmiri Pandits and Muslims. KPs have consistently and unequivocally stated that they were *driven out of their homes* by the Islamic militia and their overground sympathisers. Muslims maintain that it was Jagmohan who drove them out. To me these are the two glasses half-full. Maybe we should pour them into one.

It will be injustice on the part of Kashmir's Muslims to blame Jagmohan for everything that happened. Hundreds of incidents can be quoted as testimony, which will make it abundantly clear that militants and their overground sympathisers threatened, maimed and killed KPs in good numbers, taking into account their ratio in the population.

If some Bajrang Dal goons shout in New Delhi, *'Ek dhakka aur do, Jama masjid tod do'*, it is seen as an obvious threat to Muslims in Delhi. Shouting *'Yahan kya chalega, Nizam-e-Mustafa'* is equally tantamount to a threat for the Pandits.

It is true that militant commanders and Jamaat leaders gave and still give sermons in mosques, asking Pandits to stay back as second class citizens. In 1990, there were criminally-minded men who knocked at the doors of Pandits in the dead of night to threaten them for various reasons, other than those stated by the militants. No Kashmiri Muslim can deny that every Pandit household was threatened in one way or the other by militants or criminally minded men who had their own agenda. Most of them wanted to occupy the properties of Pandits by hounding them out.

The Pandits were first targeted by Jammu Kashmir Liberation Front (JKLF) militants. This was a time when a significant number of Pandits may have decided to side with the new narrative of Azadi. JKLF took no time in threatening them and hounding them out of the Valley. Soon Hizbul Mujahideen, backed by Jamaat-e-Islami, emerged on the scene. Cries for Nizam-e-Mustafa resonated. Was it not reason enough for the Pandits to leave? Or were they supposed to shout 'Yahan kya chalega, Nizam-e-Mustafa'?

Now for the charges that Jagmohan drove them out. I would say Mufti drove them out by engineering activities that caused them to fear for their lives. I have referred elsewhere to the comment made by the Home Secretary to the J&K government, who wished Geelani a long life because he was helping the Indian state so much. Those who drove out the Pandits did not know that they damaged the cause of Kashmir and helped the Indian state to the hilt.

Jagmohan perhaps arranged the logistics and helped the Pandits to move out of Kashmir at a point when they were totally unsafe and felt threatened.

Kashmiri Muslims cannot exonerate themselves of the responsibility that the Pandits had to leave their homeland. We should accept it, apologise for it and ask the Pandits to return back to build Kashmir collectively.

The terrorists who emerged as leaders always maintained that they were ready to welcome Pandits back with open arms. Shabir Shah was among the first few youngsters who, along with only a few of his workers, hounded Pandits out of Anantnag. Shah would later visit migrant camps in Jammu in solidarity with Pandits, and would issue statements asking them to return. Kashmiri Muslims by and large want the Kashmiri Pandits back. The political class has done politicking on the issue, and has never been serious about their return.

Kashmiris lose the Victimhood Card

THE CHANGED narratives in Kashmir, from political to religionised ones, no longer generate a positive response outside Kashmir. Love begets love, hate begets hate. The narrative of hatred has evoked negativity and at places, even hatred in the mainland towards Kashmiris.

As for the international community, the Indian government has successfully and perhaps rightfully convinced it that India is facing Islamic terrorism in Kashmir sponsored by Pakistan. Legal and moral arguments notwithstanding, the jihadists in Kashmir have damaged the legitimacy of the Kashmir struggle.

Till recently, Kashmiris would introduce themselves to the outer world as the victims of state oppression. Internationally, many would sympathise with the Kashmiris. Now it is the Indian state that projects itself as the victim of

Islamic terrorism in Kashmir, sponsored by Pakistan. There are many takers for this narrative.

The extremist Islamic narrative has destroyed the victimhood claim of the Kashmiris. *Any dialogue on giving some concessions to Kashmiris is now seen as giving concessions to extremists.* Pakistan is using jihadists in Kashmir to maintain a nationalist frenzy domestically. This is helping India in convincing the international community about the changed reality of Kashmir.

The present regime in New-Delhi is fully exploiting militancy in Kashmir for electoral benefits. The right-wing justifies its onslaught on minorities in the name of Islamic fundamentalism. If this is the situation, then we can see that both India and Pakistan have transformed the Kashmir conflict from a 'bone of contention' to a 'conflict of convenience'. Political parties in India have benefited from the Kashmir conflict by using it for further polarisation. So has Pakistan. It is only the Kashmiri who is the ultimate loser in this game. The Kashmiri has chosen the narrative that only evokes condemnation and international bashing.

In 2016, two senior Hurriyat leaders – Yasin Malik and Professor Abdul Gani Bhat – on two separate occasions expressed their satisfaction on successfully passing over the conflict to the next generation. I told Bhat that what 'you are saying with pride would make me hang my head in shame'. We Kashmiris have not been able to deal with this curse afflicting our land. We have passed it on to our children, so that they may continue to die.

When the Burhan Wani fever was at its highest after his killing, young Kashmiris would visit his mother seeking blessings for martyrdom. Once, Haj pilgrims from north

Kashmir on their way to Srinagar airport were stopped by a stone-pelting group in the city outskirts. 'The youth, mostly in 20s, told the pilgrims that they would allow them for onward journey only if they promised that they would pray for their martyrdom while performing Haj.' The incident was narrated by my friend Shujaat Bukhari to a conference in Delhi with awe. Every time I speak about this plea of Kashmiri youth, my heart bleeds that my children are so poisoned that they are choosing death over life.

In 2017, the deadly online game Blue Whale allegedly pushed some teenagers in India into committing suicide. The Indian society was alarmed. The government was forced to take measures to stop this deadly trend and banned the online game. And here, *we see Kashmir's intellectual class – the elits – glorify suicidal trends amongst its youth.*

Who has benefitted from these games of death being played in the streets of Kashmir? Kashmiri youth are killing themselves to keep intact the citadels of the mullahs who derive their legitimacy from a burning Kashmir. By strengthening the extremist narratives in Kashmir, Kashmiris are also strengthening the right-wing in the mainland.

History begins with 27 October 1947

Kashmiri teenagers invoke history whenever and wherever you start dialogue with them. They start from 27 October 1947 when the Indian troops landed in Srinagar after Maharaja Hari Singh signed the instrument of accession with the Union of India. All Kashmiris start their conversation about Kashmir from this date. They have been conditioned this way.

How many people in India are aware of the historical context of the conflict in Kashmir? Not many. There are few in mainland India with clarity on what went wrong in Kashmir. Most Indians are not even concerned with the issue.

India is a nation with a young population. Its average age is 33 years. The Indian youth have no idea of Kashmir's history. They are only familiar with terrorism, jihad, militancy and Pakistan. That is why Kashmiris are losing support in the mainland. There is a perception that the Muslim-majority Kashmir does not want to live with India or in India.

When terrorists strike elsewhere in India outside Kashmir, the Indian populace turns hostile towards Kashmir. It is understandable. The hardened extremist Islamic narrative is damaging the Kashimiri 'cause' on two fronts within India. One, the state exploits it to its strategic and political advantage. Two, public opinion turns against Kashmir and Kashmiris.

The Arabisation of Kashmir

Kashmiris have developed exclusivist tendencies, and this is a matter of serious concern. The narrative of 'us' and 'them' was successful in denting the secular and pluralist ethos of Kashmir's society. This narrative helped in shaping negative opinion about Kashmir in mainland India.

It is globally observed that Muslim societies across the world consider it a matter of right to follow the principle of religious ascendancy. In Kashmir the religious extremists have succeeded in exhibitionist religiosity. This was initially resisted by the urban class. But slowly and gradually, this has settled in. It is more about Arabisation of Kashmir society. This has left a very important segment of the society, the Kashmiri Pandits, aghast. With this Arabisation too, it is the Kashmiri Muslims who are the losers.

Since 2016, the Government of India has maintained that

the Kashmir conflict is restricted to 'two-and-a-half districts' of south Kashmir. This politically-loaded statement makes Kashmiris angry. But the statement holds merit if one sees it in context.

Let us consider the political future of the erstwhile State of Jammu and Kashmir including Gilgit and Baltistan, which is partly under the control of China. The part of Kashmir in Pakistan is not afflicted by this problem. Jammu region is predominantly Hindu. They are more than comfortable with the status quo, of remaining a part of India. Leh demands the status of union territory. That means more integration.

The problem is reduced to Kashmir Valley. In Chenab Valley and Peer Panjal region, the Muslim population has some sympathy with Kashmiris, that we are subjected to gross human rights violations by the Indian security forces. But the exclusivist ideology is restricted to Kashmir. This ideology has excluded the Valley from rest of the State. Earlier we could see some Pandit leaders identifying themselves with the political narrative of the Kashmir conflict. Now there is none.

In fact, a handful of KPs active on the Track-II front are there for monetary and other benefits. In such a context, the moral and legal argument for Kashmir has lost relevance.

The opinion leaders of Kashmir, mostly the mullahs, keep talking about the political conflict despite the fact that they have been instrumental in the transformation of Kashmir society from an inclusive, pluralist society to a radicalised one. Given the uncompromising religious narratives within Kashmir, the counter-narrative we hear is that Kashmir must be Hinduised, or its Muslim-majority demography changed. Some right-wingers suggest that ex-servicemen should be settled in Kashmir.

China Factor

China's persistent blocking of the UN resolution on designating Masood Azhar[1] as global terrorist for more than a decade (till May this year) gave it significant strategic advantage in Kashmir.

The impression that is now gaining ground is that China is the panacea to all problems in Kashmir.

All the militants and the militant groups operating in Kashmir identify themselves with Pakistan and with Pakistani militia groups. Their allegiance to Pakistan and the groups operating from its soil is acknowledged widely. And China is Pakistan's friend, Masood Azhar's friend.

One must also not forget that a portion of northern J&K, the Gilgit-Baltistan territory, occupied by Pakistan is host to a major Chinese infrastructure project. In May 2018, Pakistan attempted to exercise more control over Gilgit-Baltistan, a region that India maintains is a part of the entire State of Jammu and Kashmir and through which the $50 billion China-led CPEC project passes. The corridor links Kashgar in western China with Gwadar port in Pakistan, spanning 3,000 km. The communist nation's infrastructure push that closely mirrors its strategic ambitions is seen as one of the pain points in ties between India and China, though, theoretically, China says, the China-Pakistan Economic Corridor through Gilgit will not affect its stand that the Kashmir issue should be resolved between India and Pakistan.

By virtue of this, China has not just entered the equation in

1 Masood Azhar is the founder and leader of the Pakistan-based terrorist organisationJaish-e-Mohammed, active mainly in the Pakistani-administered portion of the State of Jammu and Kashmir. On 1 May 2019, Masood Azhar was listed as an international terrorist by United Nations Security Council. He was among those released by India during the Kandahar plane hijack incident in December 1999.

Kashmir. It has acquired a dominant position here.

The impression steadily gaining ground among Kashmiris is that Pakistan is not alone in supporting Kashmir to achieve its right to self-determination. China's might and power is militarily and diplomatically behind Pakistan. This perception is being assiduously strengthened by the local stakeholders in Kashmir. Also, this perception has emboldened the separatists.

The occasional border skirmishes between Indian and Chinese forces either in Ladakh region or elsewhere are received in Kashmir with enthusiasm. Any expression of Chinese aggression towards India is welcomed in Kashmir. It helps the terrorist groups operating in Kashmir to mobilise a higher degree of local support.

The narrative building in Kashmir in support of China is based on the old dictum, 'Enemy of the enemy is a friend'. The narrative has been consciously and convincingly constructed on the local mainstream media and social media platforms. It has been built through diverse opinion leaders like prominent civil society members, academicians, journalists and other senior professionals.

Kashmir, a landlocked society, has developed a strong 'hate India' perception. The local narrative is now strongly in favour of China. Kashmiris believe that it is China which will 'liberate them' from India. The argument is that it is China, and not Pakistan, which can crush India militarily. Hence, China is seen as the saviour of Kashmir.

Till a few years ago, the separatist constituency in Kashmir had great expectations from the US. They would invoke the US often and would attach great importance to any statement emanating from the White House vis-à-vis Kashmir. Pakistan-backed separatists would successfully lure their core constituency by invoking the US. Some separatists, particularly Jammu Kashmir Liberation Front (JKLF) chief Yasin Malik, has visited the US many times. He also developed close contacts with some government-backed think-tanks in the US. Claiming success in their communications with Americans working at some important positions, the Kashmiri separatists would always galvanise their core constituency on the US rhetoric.

In the last few years, this mechanism has, however, not worked. There has been a clear shift in geo-politics and US concerns regarding Islamist and Islamic organisations across the world.

India and US have strong diplomatic relations now. This closeness has led to a corresponding shift in Kashmir, and a change of policy at ground level. The result is Advantage China. The narrative started with China's aggression in Ladakh region and elsewhere. China's repeated sabotage of the move to designate JeM chief Masood Azhar as global terrorist was a major factor which earned it strong admiration in Kashmir.

These moves, and also China's 'iron brother' relationship with Pakistan has enthused the separatist constituency in Kashmir. It has emboldened the militant ranks operating both in Kashmir and in Pakistan. The propaganda machinery, especially the social media platforms, are actively providing fodder to this thought process. The narrative that only China can liberate Kashmir is resonating in all quarters of Kashmir. That is why China's oppression of Muslims in Xinjiang is never spoken of in Kashmir.

Integration

A more sophisticated approach has been to challenge the legality and constitutionality of Section 35A and also Article 370 in the Supreme Court. The Indian state has been systematically eroding the special position guaranteed to Jammu and Kashmir by the Constitution of India. The plan is political integration.

Kashmiri Muslims have failed to understand that the other state subjects – the Dogras of Jammu and the Buddhists of Ladakh – all want integration with India. Why?

Essentially because the Kashmiri leadership, both in the mainstream and the separatist camp, have failed to take non-Muslims of the State's other two regions on board. If you look at the problem through this perspective, the Kashmir problem is restricted to just two-and-a-half districts.

The phenomenon of Islamism has dealt a blow to Kashmiris within the State, and also nationally and internationally. Ashraf Sehrai, on assuming the charge of the Geelani faction of the Hurriyat, realised the damage caused to the Kashmir cause by Islamisation. He tried to give the impression that he would redefine the narratives, but soon he got tangled in a peculiar situation. As I noted earlier, within days of his taking over charge, his son Junaid joined Hizbul Mujahideen.

Pakistan is happy with the radical Islamist narrative in Kashmir.

India is building its victim position through Kashmir's radical Islamism, both locally and globally. BJP won the 2019 elections with a thumping majority only on Kashmir and Pakistan.

Jammu region wants to integrate with the Union of India. Ladakh wants to be a union territory. It is only the Kashmiri Muslims who are consumed in the conflict of convenience.

An oft-repeated argument is that the Kashmir's society as a whole is a peace-loving society. It does not endorse the violent form of Islam:

> It is a conspiracy against Kashmiri Muslims to label them as radicals. The argument holds forth that we are fighting Indian state's oppression. The state didn't respond to our struggle through peaceful means. It is argued that we are forced by the state to take to guns and stones, as there is no scope for peaceful means of protest in India.
>
> The argument further is that we have exhausted all options to pressurise India to come to the negotiating table and accept our plea for self-determination. Then there comes the statement which Kashmiris often quote: Mahatma Gandhi said in 1947 that he saw a beam of light in Kashmir when the entire subcontinent was in flames, burning in communal fire.

Kashmiris refuse to accept that the clock is not stuck in 1947. The Kashmiri leadership of those times had realised the dangers of communalism and religionism long before the debacle of Partition. They named the Muslim Conference as National Conference way back in 1938. Their sagacity paid off in 1947.

If your detractor or oppressor is not responding to your peaceful struggle, does that mean that you will resort to violence? Even if you resort to violence by acquiring guns from your oppressor's enemy, does that mean you will dump your peaceful, secular and pluralistic narratives, and adopt narratives drawn from medieval ages? If that is the case, you are providing more ground to your enemy to oppress you.

Sheikh Abdullah did not endorse violence as a means to achieve the goals envisioned for Kashmir. If the Kashmiris took to arms in 1989, it was again the so-called leadership which waged the war in Kashmir at the cost of innocent people. Initially, they sold dreams at the cost of a peaceful life. Later, they sold fantasies of jannat (heaven) and enthused, instigated, indoctrinated unsuspecting teenagers to leave earth for the heavenly abode – the sooner the better.

Someone has to be accountable for the tragic mess that our lives have become. I strongly believe that the Indian state infringed upon our rights. It always looked upon us with suspicion. It relentlessly pursued the systematic and systemic integration of Jammu and Kashmir without caring for our sentiments. With all this, I cannot justify the path of violence adopted by us.

See how the fantasies of jannat are sold to the youth in Kashmir. In early 2018, some teenagers were killed in Syria following air strikes by the American forces. It was a heart-wrenching incident that shook the conscience of people globally. During the same time, six civilians (stone pelters) got killed in an encounter in south Kashmir's Khudwani area while they were trying to give safe passage to trapped militants. They succeeded in their endeavour.

Soon thereafter, a Facebook post went viral in Kashmir. It went like this: There was a ruckus in Heaven yesterday when 20 Syrian teenaged martyrs and six Kashmiri martyrs reached there. Hoors were singing and praising our martyrs. Heaven was shining in their reception.

Take note, the Government in Kashmir as well as the Government of India allowed Facebook to maintain this post online.

When young impressionable youth are bombarded with this messaging, what does our society expect? But our leaders are still in denial mode. They do not accept that Kashmir, which was once a plural, peace-loving society has been destroyed beyond redemption. If there is agreement, it is only to the extent of cautioning India that if it does not shun the path of rigidity, things will be difficult for it to handle.

The Narrative of Intolerance

Kashmir's radical transformation must be a matter of serious concern for the Indian state and the people of India. The Government of India cannot afford to undermine the dangers of the growing intolerant extremist narrative in Kashmir. This will not remain confined to the borders of Kashmir alone. The current phase of violence has strong ideological foundations. It has the potential to damage the rest of the country, starting with the neighbouring States.

The State administration has continued its ostrich-like approach to the problem. This will have devastating consequences. Kashmir has been damaged totally. It has been handed over to illiterate clerics and violent mobs. The damage is irreparable, both in terms of conflict resolution and the rupture of the social fabric.

Many liberals, Leftists and secularists in the mainland have realised that they cannot justify the violence in Kashmir any more, since it has taken new dimensions based on religious ideology.

The hardened narratives in Kashmir have left the liberals shocked. In the last four to five years, I have approached many of them to come to Kashmir and interact with the youth. Many liberal secularists do not want to be identified with the current dominant narratives in Kashmir.

Political discourse in India has shifted right-ward. Labels of anti-national, pro-Pakistan, anti-India, anti-Hindu are handed out fast and thick. It is a repeat of what moderates in Kashmir who tried to ring alarm bells at the ugly transformation of the society, suffered for years. Anti-Kashmir, anti-Muslim, anti-Islam, apostate, Indian agent.

Hartal and Bandhs: Self-inflicting Agonies

HUSAIN HAQQANI wrote in July 2003 that Pakistan lacks an endgame for Kashmir. It has acted through military incursions, terrorism and appeals for international support that have increasingly fallen on deaf ears.

The Kashmir 'movement' is the result of Pakistan's flawed policy. The so-called leadership still has no idea about how to end this game, or even how to respond to situations. Kashmir's separatist leadership is devoid of any strategy for the Valley, and no out-of-box thinking. They cannot think beyond giving frequent calls for *hartals* or strikes. Nor can they think imaginatively about participation in the electoral process.

In 2002, Jamaat-e-Islami tacitly and tactically supported Mufti's PDP to capture power. Except this one time, their only tool since 1990 has been to call for boycotting the elections

– both to the State legislature and the Indian parliament. Elections are held in Kashmir with or without the participation of the electorate.

Have the endless calls for hartal and boycott given by the separatists helped the Kashmir cause in any way? Is there any outcry in international forums about the 'disenchantment' of Kashmiris with electoral politics? No. How has the politics of the separatists impacted Kashmir's economy and its evolution politically?

These questions are not being asked yet. The prevailing fear snuffs out any efforts at discussions in Kashmir.

The boycott call was first given in 1994. The logic given by the separatists was that it would attract the attention of the international community and force them to intervene for resolving the conflict. It was claimed that the international clamour would impress upon the Indian state to resolve the issue. We now know that *boycott politics has drawn zero international scrutiny.*

In 2016, Pakistan Prime Minister Nawaz Sharif spoke in the UN Security Council about the plight of the Kashmiris and their 'inalienable right to self-determination'. The 184 member states did not show any interest. The world media did not refer to Sharif's speech even remotely the next day.

If this is the situation, why don't the Kashmir separatists change their strategy? In June 2018, the UN Human Rights Commission released a report, accusing the Indian state of committing serious human rights violations in Kashmir. The Indian government rejected the report even without discussing it officially. Is this the kind of global intervention that the separatists in Kashmir are vouching for?

In November 2010, US president Barack Obama visited

India at a time when Kashmir was engulfed by violence. About 120 people, mostly teenagers, had lost their lives in street protests. The hartal calendar (as it is called in Kashmir) was being issued on a weekly basis by Syed Ali Geelani.

Obama landed in Mumbai. The next day he visited Delhi, where he addressed a press conference. He did not utter even a word on the prevailing situation in Kashmir. During his presser, a scribe questioned him on the strained relations between India and Pakistan. Obama responded that India and Pakistan should resolve their long-pending issues between them peacefully through dialogue.

The next day, Geelani issued a statement saying that the sacrifices made by Kashmiris will not go waste. He said that the remarks made by Obama regarding Kashmir were the result of the '120 sacrifices we made during this year'.

I was aghast at this statement and wrote an open letter to Geelani in a local Urdu daily. I reminded Geelani that Obama had not uttered a single word regarding Kashmir during his two-day visit to India. He responded to a scribe's question on the strained relations between India and Pakistan without any specific reference to Kashmir.

I asked Geelani in the open letter: If you consider that Obama responded because of the 120 lives we lost in street protests against Indian forces, please tell us what did Kashmir gain from the one lakh sacrifices (Geelani's figure) made so far? If 120 lives lost in street protests made Obama comment on 'long pending issues', what would it take for him to act on the one lakh sacrifices made by Kashmiris?

The debate over the boycott politics of the separatists has lost relevance, given the emergence of dominant extremist narratives in Kashmir. Boycott politics had lost relevance long ago. The Indian state has been naïve in celebrating the participation of Kashmiris in elections as a referendum against separatism and Pakistan. Perhaps this illogical and irresponsible narrative may have dissuaded the Kashmir separatists from revisiting boycott politics. But boycott politics cannot be the mantra forever. The poor voter turnout in Kashmir has dented the credibility of electoral politics in Kashmir. But this news has not mattered beyond Pakistan. The international community is mute and does not respond to such developments on account of the changing narratives.

Many Faces of the Elections Sphynx

Kashmiri separatists have played and sold boycott politics locally. Boycott politics has encouraged the socially and morally discredited fringe to exploit the situation to its advantage. Let us take the recently-held Panchayat and local body elections. BJP claims that 1,800 *panches*,[2] sarpanches and councilors of the saffron party won in Kashmir Valley. How is it possible that BJP could make inroads in Kashmir politics to such a significant level? NC and PDP boycotted the elections. BJP fielded candidates in large numbers who won unopposed because there was no contest at all.

One can analyse the elections held in Kashmir 1990 onwards. At many places, credible faces could not enter the fray because of the boycott announced by the separatists. At times, this resulted in the victory of socially discredited elements.

In 1997, a friend invited me for lunch to his house in a remote village in south Kashmir. It was Friday. Before having lunch, my friend took me to the mosque to offer Friday

---

2 local councilors.

congregational prayers. It was shocking to find that the man delivering the sermon was a maniac. I was puzzled to see a guy who seemed mad, delivering the sermon to about 1,000 men. They were listening to him without any sign of discomfort. After the prayers got over, I shouted at my friend, 'You forced me to listen to a psychopath. He was not representing any school of thought. He was a maniac. Shame on you that your entire village was sitting there, listening to him without feeling uncomfortable'. My friend retorted, 'It was shame on you, not me. When serious scholars like you leave the podium vacant, someone will take their space, be it a psychopath'.

I felt ashamed. He was right. Over the years, boycott politics has forced wise, politically mature people to withdraw, fearing threat to their lives and families. Maniacs have jumped in and occupied the space.

Our elected representatives have the legitimacy, legally and constitutionally, to represent us. They brave the threats of the separatists. On this account I admire them. But we also have the emergence of a section on the political landscape which has lowered the level of representation intellectually and politically.

In Pahalgam constituency, I knew a man named Abdul Khaliq Reshi. He worked as the assistant of a senior lawyer in the district court at Anantnag. Reshi was poor, but a good orator and a sharp political worker. In the 2008 assembly elections, there was a triangular contest in Pahalgam between PDP, NC and Congress. Reshi had worked with all the three candidates in the past.

One day Reshi created a record of sorts. First, he was part of a public meeting of the NC candidate at Aishmuqam village. He gave an electrifying speech while sharing the stage with the NC candidate. After his speech, he left hurriedly. He went to the other side of Lidder river, where the PDP candidate was supposed to address the voters. Reshi joined him. In a thundering speech, he urged the voters to support the PDP candidate.

Soon he left the stage and went rushing to another village, where the Congress candidate was flexing his muscles. Reshi comfortably joined him on the stage and relaxed for some time. Then he delivered a passionate speech, asking the voters of Pahalgam constituency to ensure the victory of the Congress candidate. He was a poor man struggling to earn something for his family.

Once a political worker, who was a National Conference worker by birth and conviction, showed me four identity cards. One was the delegate card allotted to him by NC. The other was a PDP worker card with the signature of Mehbooba Mufti. The third card was from Tehreek Hurriyat of Syed Ali Geelani. The fourth was his voter identity card.

I have met scores of such Kashmiri men who are workers of two or three political parties simultaneously. Jammu region is influenced by national politics and prefers to be part of the larger national discourse. Political parties and candidates mobilise crowds for public meeting, rallies and protests by giving money. This was not the case with mainstream politics in Kashmir till 2000. People would come to public meetings out of conviction or curiosity, but money played no role.

After the separatists started giving money to their workers for mobilisation, the mainstream too resorted to the money game. A section of the society emerged as floaters. They came for money, whoever gave it. We have had instances where the same man was in charge of mobilisation for two political leaders, if not two political parties.

Boycott and hartal politics has seriously damaged Kashmir's development. Because of frequent strikes which have sometimes lasted for months, funds allocated for developmental works in Kashmir division under various sectors are never utilised during the particular fiscal year. To avoid lapse of funds, in many cases the government diverts the funds to other division – the Jammu division – in the last quarter of the fiscal year for utilisation till 31 March. This way, funds for Kashmir leave its landscape.

December onwards, Kashmir faces a harsh winter, when work on developmental projects get hampered due to freezing temperature. The weather remains pleasant in Jammu during winter months. Hence good use of funds can be made for developmental works there.

The separatists do not allow developmental works to take place during summer by issuing strike calls which cripple normal life. These same forces raise a hue and cry over the diversion of funds to Jammu region. A narrative of discrimination is constructed, and a conspiracy theory is attributed to this simple financial rule.

Election bells have started ringing. The nation has voted. Kashmir too is in election mood. By election mood, I mean both boycott and voting. The boycott call from the separatists is expected anytime. Geelani has already issued a statement, asking people not to affiliate with the mainstream parties. The impact of his call depends on the threats perceived by the people due to the enforcement of the boycott call by the militants.

The severity of the boycott may be felt more this year. Militants have to make their presence felt. They may go on a killing spree, particularly in south Kashmir. Administrative machinery and the law enforcement agencies are struggling for the smooth conduct of the upcoming assembly elections and the participation of the electorate. The separatists and the poll boycott enforcement forces are equally at work, trying their best to keep people away from exercising their franchise.

Boycott politics and violence go side by side. Tragically, new casualties will take place, and many voices may be silenced.

Why do the separatists want that Kashmiris should not exercise their electoral franchise? Kashmir's mainstream and separatist political leaders have maintained for decades that elections cannot change the nature of the Kashmir dispute. Some Kashmiri political leaders have also admitted that boycotting the elections could have been an option if it fetched the desired results, or if it helped in resolving the problem.

Rigged and Fair

Syed Ali Geelani had contested in the infamous rigged election of 1987. He and other separatists now masquerade as boycott generals. The 1987 election is regarded as a turning point in the history of Kashmir, forcing Kashmiris to go to the other side of the border and get arms training.

But it is also widely agreed that 1987 saw the last rigged election in the political history of Jammu and Kashmir.

Rigging of elections, which amounts to disrespecting people's mandate and muzzling their voice, could have given sanctity to boycott politics. This was one of the reasons why in 1996, people largely boycotted the assembly elections in Kashmir. Fear of militants was also looming large.

It is widely believed that though participation in the 1996 election was low, the elections were fair.

The elections in 2002 reinforced people's faith in the electoral process.

In 2008, the assembly election in J&K threw up a fractured

mandate, with PDP as a loser. Tariq Hameed Karra, who was then a PDP leader (he recently joined the Congress), kept shouting in party meetings that the elections were tactically rigged.

PDP leader Mufti Mohd Sayeed never endorsed Karra. Mufti, as also the rest of Kashmir, believed that the elections were free and fair, and that these were a vote for change. Even hardcore supporters of election boycott will agree that at least since 2002, elections conducted in Jammu and Kashmir have been free and fair.

Then why should Kashmiris boycott the elections?

One rigged election forced a section of the leadership and the youth to pit themselves against the state. Why can't a series of free and fair elections make them turn around and change course? The fact is: the people turned around, but their leaders could not. Kashmiris put their faith in electoral democracy, though they also kept harbouring impractical political ambitions.

Boycott politics has two dimensions. One, the separatists themselves reject the test of electoral politics. Two, they ask people to stay away from polling booths and not exercise their franchise.

The Indian media and Kashmir's mainstream political parties have argued for two decades that *Kashmiri separatists are afraid of electoral drubbing*. They fear that people will reject them.

PDP MP Muzaffar Baig recently stated what a sizable majority of Kashmiris have known for long. Baig said the separatists have consistently inflicted miseries on people and thrived on the dead bodies of Kashmiris.

Some Kashmiris have begun to ask this question. That – in order to protect themselves from a deplorable electoral fate which will expose their true credentials, will the separatists keep on leading the Kashmiris, particularly the youth, to their death? Will they keep on vitiating the atmosphere, dismantle the inclusive Kashmiri ethos, and destroy the social fabric only to satisfy their egos?

We know that the elections have not been able to change the nature of the Kashmir dispute. If the elections are only about *bijli sadak paani*, why do the separatists deny people their democratic rights?

The separatists, who claim to be fighting for the rights of the people of Kashmir, are denying the rights extended to the people of Kashmir by the Indian Constitution. Their so-called movement cannot be seen as a movement for rights.

Even more dangerous is the enforcement of boycott. It is like the anti-militancy crackdowns in the '90s by the armed forces in villages across Kashmir. One could not dare to ask for a glass of water. Nobody was spared. Everyone had to follow the diktat of the men conducting the crackdown or get killed.

Following the call for poll boycott, militants will target poor, unprotected political workers, former panches and sarpanches and sympathisers of political parties. The situation is tragic indeed.

After 2002, Kashmiris rejected the boycott call of the separatists. Kashmiris are ambitious, aspirational people. Resolution of the Kashmir dispute has been their ardent wish. With the elections, they seek resolution of their immediate civic issues. These are mostly Kashmiris above 30.

An alarming section of Kashmiris below 30 think differently. They are alienated and radicalised. For them, participation in elections is treason. They regard those who exercise their franchise as apostates, more or less.

Violence, Religious Bigotry eating up Kashmir

THE JAMMU and Kashmir State is as complex a political and geographical entity as its conflict. After the inception of the violent phase of turmoil, the State has witnessed an interesting imbalance in competitive examinations.

For decades, Jammuites had accused the Kashmir-centric political parties of discrimination in the employment of youth in the public sector. Jammu-based political and religious groups always smelled foul in the selection of candidates for the civil services and other public sector employment programmes. These accusations have never been substantiated by evidence. The BJP was leading this narrative. With their coming to power in 2014, the narrative slowed down, but other groups still continue with it.

Of course, successive governments in Jammu and Kashmir routinely resort to backdoor appointments for Class IV jobs in government and public sector undertakings. Ministers and political leaders accommodate their workers through backdoor channels to keep their vote banks intact. This cannot be seen as discrimination against a particular region, because these appointments have always been constituency centric. This has been true about all ministers, regardless of the region they come from.

In the civil services, it was commonly believed that Kashmiri students outsmarted their counterparts from Jammu region. In the Civil Secretariat, most departments were usually headed by Kashmiri civil servants, whether Muslims or Pandits. The instinct of competition was inculcated among Kashmiri Muslims by Kashmiri Pandits. From 1960 to 1988, Kashmiri Pandits were mostly in the teaching profession. They encouraged students of the Valley to compete academically and professionally with honesty and dedication. Every Kashmiri aged 40 or more will give credit to Kashmiri Pandits for the ever-increasing literacy rate of Kashmiri Muslims, and also for encouraging them to compete at State and national level. The result was that Kashmiri Muslims cracked the civil services and other combined services examinations in large numbers.

With this, bureaucracy in Jammu and Kashmir had a significant percentage of Kashmiris. The same was true about government services in Class II and Class III grade. Students from rural Kashmir would outnumber their counterparts coming from the urban areas. Their zeal and triumph tilted the ratio of bureaucracy in the State, and naturally, Jammuites raised the slogan of discrimination. The hue and cry was political, and far from reality.

Things changed as religious bigotry and radicalism spread in rural Kashmir. Two developments took place simultaneously – the advent of radical Islam and the exodus of Kashmiri pandits. The Islamists, particularly Jamaat-e-Islami, adopted the mantle of saviour of Islam. According to them, this meant that Islam was under threat from secularists and Indians. With the increasing number of militants from radical organisations, the legitimisation of Jamaat became inevitable. *Jamaat established Sharia courts across the length and breadth of Kashmir Valley for resolving the civil and even criminal disputes in accordance with the Sharia.*

The jurists at these courts, who were supposed to invoke Islamic Jurisprudence in matters of civil and criminal disputes, were mostly illiterates. Rural areas hardly attract media attention. This provided greater leeway to the Jamaatis in rural Kashmir. After Islamic extremism, terrorism struck roots in rural Kashmir. Innocent teenagers who would have excelled in various fields became victims of indoctrination by the Jamaat. They lost interest in 'material life', and strove hard to make their 'hereafter' better, and thereby sacrificed this earthly world.

An important aspect of the legitimisation of Jamaat and its poisonous extremist ideology was that several so-called mainstream political parties, groups and individuals sought their support. Even after it was banned by the government, Jamaat continued its work via obscure and unfamiliar organisations, trusts and charities.

The continuing persecution of non-Jamaatis and violation of human rights of those opposing religious bigotry became the hallmark of post-1990 Jamaat-e-Islami in Kashmir. More and more youth in schools and colleges identified themselves with Jamaat – both within and outside madrasas.

Watching the Jamaat feeding on green pastures in the countryside, religious bigots from other schools of thought like the Deobandi, Wahabi, Tabhleegi – all went into competing mode for opening madrasas all over Kashmir. The competition for a better future was replaced by competition for a heavenly life.

With the influence of radical Islam in Kashmir, the administrative and civil services ratio started tilting in favour of the Jammu region. There was an additional reason for this. After their exodus from the Valley, a large number of Kashmiri Pandits settled in Jammu. Kashmiri Pandits had taken the lead in the field of education since centuries. They encouraged competition in Jammu the same way they used to in Kashmir. Youth from the Pandit community mingled with the Dogras of Jammu. This promoted competition in the field of education.

The result was that youth from Jammu started cracking civil, judiciary and other services examinations in large numbers. Kashmiris, meanwhile, started looking at every development with suspicion. Conspiracy theories were thrown about in abundance.

Now it is Kashmir that cries foul for almost all the combined services examinations, alleging unfair means and conspiracy by the people at the helm. A significant percentage of them are now non-Kashmiris.

Back in Kashmir, the competition between producing more and more clerics and religious preachers ensued between various schools of thought. *The ground situation in the countryside is that in every village, a new breed of religious clerics is seen in scores. The existing network of mosques could not accommodate all the clerics produced in madrasas. Hence new mosques are coming up in hundreds. Every sect is building mosques in every habitation.*

It is interesting to watch that *government institutions are promoting the same culture,* ostensibly to adjust with the changing ground realities. *The ambience in government schools is Islamic now.* Customs, rituals, mannerisms, invocations – all are Islamic. Online content has played a pivotal role in radicalising the youth. *One cannot differentiate in the morning which student is going to the government school, and which one to a madrasa, because the ambience at both places is the same. The situation is such that you don't know what the children in schools, colleges and universities are up to.*

My elder son was in the last semester of his engineering degree in electronics at NIT Srinagar. He is a gifted young man. Sharp, intelligent and wise. In our village, he was seen as a role model for other children. My bureaucrat friends would say that he would be the next Shah Faesal from Kashmir.

In September 2014, I was sitting with my laptop in the afternoon, doing some news-story for a local newspaper. Suddenly a new mail dropped in. It was from my son. He had mailed me a video with the remark, 'Watch this video Abbu. It will change your outlook'.

I started playing the video. It was the sermon of some foreign Islamic scholar. I called my wife who was working in the kitchen. She watched the video for a few minutes and asked me who had sent it. I told her, 'The video has been sent by our late son'. She shouted at me, 'How dare you use such harsh language! My son is in good health, why are you saying late!' I gently told her that of course her son was fit and fine with the grace of God, but unfortunately my son in him had died.

After completing the last semester, he returned home. He was completely changed. His beard was longer now. His salwar had shortened. He had no inclination to appear for civil services.

He was content reading the namaz and reciting the Quran.

Our neighbours started calling him Moulvi Saab. They said I was very fortunate that such a young man was my son. 'He is on the right path. God has bestowed love upon him. He will serve Islam and earn jannat for you too', they told me. A neighbour who is my good friend and has a Jamaat background got him appointed as deputy imam of the local mosque. This neighbour has three daughters and a son. His two daughters have government jobs. The third one is doing PhD at the University of Agricultural Sciences and Technology, Kashmir. His son has done engineering and is preparing for competitive examinations.

Watching my elder son, I felt broken.

My clan expressed anguish over me. They approved his Islamisation and called me an infidel for attempting to ensure that he should not squander his youth and his life to indoctrination. It took my son three years to come out of the stupor of indoctrination.

Most Kashmiri parents who face a similar situation approve their children's Islamisation. You never know what will happen next as far as your children are concerned. I myself was influenced by Jamaat ideology in the prime of my youth, and there was no one to save me. When I emerged from the deeply indoctrinated stage, I found myself staring at uncertainty in life. I used to be a topper. My parents, teachers – everyone had pinned hopes on me. The Jamaat influence and the years I lost to this ideology shattered everything.

We fail to see who is destroying our future generations.

We believe that those who indoctrinate and radicalise our children are the saviours of Islam. People will argue that despite all odds, our children are good at education. Students of south

Kashmir are scoring higher than students in Srinagar.

I agree that students in Kashmir Valley are doing well in examinations conducted by the JK State Board of Education. But indoctrination makes them vulnerable. It is this indoctrination that is making educated and qualified youth take to arms. We are fast losing our invaluable human resource to violence and radicalisation.

In the last two years, we have seen girls taking to street protests against the security forces, throwing stones and raising slogans of Nizam-e-Mustafa. These are our children, getting consumed by deadly ideologies. They are not on the path of war with the state. *They are raising their voice for creating a state of Islam in Kashmir.* No one is stopping them because no one wants to be declared an infidel and apostate.

Meanwhile, demography in government offices is changing. In the process of fighting for our rights, we have lost everything to the deadly conflict. Kashmir continues to nurture the narrative 'Islam in danger'. The gradual shift of focus from conflict resolution to Islamisation has eaten up the vitals of Kashmir's society. It has reduced the prospects of empowerment of Kashmiris.

The Mirror has Two Sides

Alienation, anger, frustration and Islamisation has eaten up the vitals of Kashmir society. Nevertheless, we remain a strongly aspirational society. A sizable section of our youth are still futuristic. They want to compete globally in education, science, arts and performing arts, music and all other areas of human knowledge.

In 2000, Abdul Gani Lone told me to convey to Geelani that Kashmiris are not Afghans. We have aspirations. We want better amenities. We want better education for our children. We cannot live in permanent war. Of course, we have political ambitions, but we simultaneously thirst for a better life.

This observation still holds good. We frequently come across news reports about Kashmiris who have excelled at sports, ranked high in the UPSC exams and so on. Simultaneously, we also have reports of educated youth joining militant ranks. Soon, their images in military fatigues and holding guns go viral in the Valley. Both things go side by side.

While encounters are going on in one part of the Kashmir Valley, in some part of Kashmir you will find a sports stadium full, with youth in large numbers watching and participating in sports activity. Kashmir is a complex society. You cannot identify it with any one thing. The problem is that the entire younger generation is vulnerably placed. This is a generation filled with hatred for 'them'. They are attracted towards some glorified, mythical and mystical medieval period. This hatred for 'them' – The Other – and severe religionisation has put Kashmir society in reverse gear. Instead of moving forward with scientific acumen and outlook, Kashmir society is fast losing to competition.

Shah Faesal topped the Indian Administrative Services examination. He reached the heights of name and fame. He resigned to join politics. But politics has no scope in Kashmir. In 2004, I had written in an article that in a conflict zone, politics is subservient to external factors and forces. Nothing indigenous exists in a conflict zone. Everything is imported.

With severe religionisation of the society, Kashmiri youth can easily be instigated or indoctrinated to search for eternal life in death. Such a state of mind is an abnormality among blossoming youth. It is a sign that the society has derailed.

Shrinking of Space for Mainstream Politics

SINCE 1990, there is a debate going on in Kashmir about the 'shrinking space' of mainstream politics. Not only writers and opinion makers but also political leaders including the Abdullahs and Muftis have been talking about the squeezing of space for mainstream politics.

In 2010 and 2012, Mufti Mohammed Sayeed and Mehbooba Mufti would fret and fume that due to mis-governance and mishandling of issues by then chief minister Omar Abdullah, the space for mainstream politics had shrunk. Omar Abdullah returned the favour in 2016 and 2017, when Mehbooba was chief minister. Other politicians of Kashmir occasionally voice their concerns on similar lines.

The separatist camp and their sympathisers use this same vocabulary against the mainstream to make their point. Shah

Faesal, who resigned from the IAS recently, chose the word 'delegitimisation'. A political commentator, who had retired from government service in Kashmir about a decade ago and writes regularly in a vernacular daily, invoked history to prove his point that political space was never made available in Kashmir.

As I have discussed in a separate chapter, retired government servants are a class apart. *The system is fine* when they were in service, drawing perks and were part of the well-oiled network of corruption and nepotism. As soon as they retire, they discover that *the system is rotten* and the state brutal.

I admire Shah Faesal for taking this monumental decision of resigning from the IAS. If he says political space was never available in Kashmir, I may have reason to believe him. But a person who had not even qualified KAS and rose to the IAS cadre through promotions asks Omar Abdullah to look into history and see if his grandfather signed on the dotted lines. This I cannot abide and think, such retired opportunists should sit at home and undertake some much-needed introspection.

In 2009, during the times I was with Mufti Mohammed Sayeed, Geelani issued some statement mildly attacking the Muftis for something. I don't remember what it was about. Mufti called me to his residence. He looked disturbed and had the newspaper in his hand. 'Geelani Saab has criticised us', Mufti said to me. As he was speaking, his lifetime advisor, Nayeem Akhtar, walked in.

I told Mufti, 'You have constructed a powerhouse on flood waters. Once the water recedes, your powerhouse will dry up in darkness'. Mufti got angry. 'What do you mean?' he asked me. I told Mufti, 'You need to build your own organisation. How long will you survive on this soft separatism? Tomorrow the situation may take some unexpected turn, and Jamaat can turn its back on you'.

Nayeem downplayed me and said, 'We know what we are doing'.

In Kashmir, mainstream space has not been squeezed, it has been surrendered. National Conference is the only cadre-based organisation in Kashmir. It has failed to connect to the generation of conflict.

No Future Perfect Plans

Given the toxicity sown in the minds of the youth regarding Sheikh Abdullah, it is certainly a challenge for NC to connect to this generation. But what is the driving force for the youth to connect? *The NC leadership still believes that the autonomy plank will fetch votes for the party.* I don't see that happening.

The mainstream, when in power, is plagued by corruption and nepotism. In or out of power, it has not been able to present a futuristic agenda before the youth in Kashmir. In the absence of opportunities, the youth turn to mosques for heavenly intervention.

How can we help in channelising Kashmir's youth towards mainstream? One, don't sell them dreams. A bourgeois leftist once asked me, 'How will you describe, rather define Mufti?' I told him, 'Mufti is a person who never means what he says and never says what he means'. This is the problem with the Kashmir mainstream. It holds true for the Abdullahs too.

If the Kashmir conflict comes in the way of stating the truth, the Kashmir mainstream has the fundamental responsibility to build consensus in the regions and religions of the State. Instead of proposing roadmaps to New Delhi, the priority should be on building consensus among all the three regions of Jammu and Kashmir.

It is essential to educate the youth about the fact that Jammu and Kashmir has to stay as a single political entity.

Hence evolving consensus among the people of all the regions and religions is fundamental to the resolution of the conflict. India-Pakistan friction apart, the opposite narratives coming from Jammu and Ladakh are the biggest impediments in the resolution process. Can Omar muster the courage? I don't know whether he can, despite the fact that NC still has some space in Jammu region, and Farooq's charismatic leadership could be the rallying point.

Shah Faesal has a clean slate. Perhaps he can work in this direction. Right-wingers fret about each other and feed each other. In building consensus lies the death of many businesses in both Jammu and Kashmir. The business of guns, the business of mosques, the business of drugs, the business of politics.

But this needs to be done. We need to build bridges which have been demolished over the years both by Kashmir's mainstream, particularly Mehbooba and the separatists, and the right-wing Hindus of Jammu. In December 2016, I told a conference in Bengaluru that *if you want to bring Srinagar close to Delhi, bring Jammu close to Srinagar. This is right both politically and strategically. It will create more space for the mainstream parties in Kashmir.*

The mainstream in Kashmir must be aggressive rather than apologetic. The inner strength to be aggressive must flow from history itself. The same history which is being selectively and subjectively propagated by the antagonists in Kashmir. *The NC leadership shoulders a huge responsibility in presenting history in the correct perspective.*

In 2017, Muzaffer Husain Beg and Engineer Rashid were on a TV show. Rashid invoked the UN resolutions on Kashmir. Beg put the resolutions in perspective and said that the resolutions were impracticable because of the conditions attached to them. Rashid immediately responded that Pakistan has to fulfill the conditions then.

The problem with the Kashmir mainstream is they never speak from the position of strength. Is it because of the huge burden of mis-governance that they carry? Are they restrained by electoral benefits? Or both?

The Indian state should also have taken an argumentatively strong position in addressing Kashmir. The Indian government has always invoked the *atoot ang*[3] phraseology but has never argued how Kashmir is an *atoot ang*. The Indian state's aggression and the Kashmir mainstream's softness has led to shrinking space for mainstream politics in Kashmir.

Kinship Politics

Another important factor is the centralisation of political parties. The people who swear by democracy never allow democratisation within their parties. The culture of dynasty politics is now reflected at ground level too, with political workers promoting their sons and daughters wherever they can. Where is the space for educated, talented and ambitious youth to prove themselves in the political field?

In every nook and corner of Kashmir Valley and across the political spectrum, the political class is promoting kinship politics. Top leaders approve this model. There are dynasties in the mainstream and the separatist camp alike. The culture of kinship promotion is phenomenal in Kashmir. This culture has also narrowed down the space for mainstream politics.

Nepotism has disenchanted the politically ambitious youth.

---

3 undivided, unbroken limb

There are hundreds of such instances where the youth who were part of a mainstream political party shifted to separatism in disenchantment, because they were not given space. On the Kashmir social media, I am often surprised to see a number of youths, who till yesterday were affiliated to a mainstream political party, spreading venom against the same party. When I examined the reasons for this pattern, I was amazed to find that blatant kinship promotion by the political class had made these youth drift away.

The political class on both sides of the divide has nurtured family fiefdom. Every single member of this class wants to see his son or daughter carrying forward his legacy. A leftist political heavyweight in south Kashmir tried hard to promote his adopted son. The son stammered and could not speak smoothly. He could not establish a connect with the electorate.

In the '90s, the threat posed by the militants to politically ambitious individuals paradoxically strengthened family fiefdoms. Since the political class was protected, they wanted to launch their relatives in politics and extend the same cocoon of power and security to them. In Srinagar district, Tariq Hameed Karra, a PDP leader, launched his wife, sister-in-law and two more relatives from four out of nine assembly segments in 2008.

Whenever assembly elections will be held in Kashmir, dozens of sons and daughters of politicians cutting across parties will get ready ready to strike it big politically. And aspirants who don't enjoy political patronage will again be seen leaving the mainstream in protest, which further leads to alienation and anger. This vicious cycle must end.

The Numbness is Deep in Kashmir

AS I decided to wrap up this book, the news of a 25-year-old woman abducted and killed by militants in Shopian district came in. This was followed by the disturbing news about seven youth gone missing from Budgam, Shopian, Pulwama, Kulgam and Anantnag districts. It was feared that they may have joined militancy.

The militants made a video of the barbaric killing of the young woman and circulated it. It went viral. Ahmad Ali Fayyaz, a senior Srinagar journalist, tweeted a Kashmiri couplet and its translation. 'Who do you expect to raise his voice against a murder? Someone has just dropped the body on the dark alley to bludgeon us all into silence.'

The numbness is deep in Kashmir. People have become mute spectators of barbarity. One, the sheer fear of death.

Fayyaz referred to the same in his tweet. Second, many among the elderly Kashmiris are aghast to see these videos of death being celebrated. The generation of conflict is harsh. It shares the videos on social media sites to celebrate the killing of an 'informer'. The informer is labeled an 'infidel'. This happens not in Pakhtoonkhwa, nor in Afghanistan, but in India-administered Kashmir, with *both the State government and GoI allowing internet connectivity for such terrorising.*

Kashmiri politicians and religious leaders have moved the burden of the conflict to shoulders of the young generation. They didn't shift inclusivity and the value of tolerance. The youth are not to be blamed. *Today, no religious scholar in Kashmir will condemn this barbarism. Those who dared to do so were silenced a long time ago.*

Now, religious scholars and the commoners alike put the blame squarely on the victim. Religious leaders, both illiterate and educated, justify the killings perpetrated by the militants. *Kashmir shuts for several days following any barbaric action of the security forces. Men, women, children – all come out to protest all inhuman killings by the security forces. Indeed, they should.*

But why does everyone fall silent when such acts are carried out by militants? Does it mean that we approve such killings? If that is the case, we cannot claim to be innocent.

In January 2005, a conference was organised at Jamia Milia Islamia, Delhi, by the Nelson Mandela Chair, which was then headed by Radha Kumar. Some Pakistani guests were also participating in the conference. There were about 20 participants from Jammu and Kashmir, including politicians, lawyers and civil society members. I was among them.

We were in the middle of the conference when we received the news that MLA MY Tarigami's nephew had been killed by militants. Tarigami was among the participants at the conference. Soon, he left the conference hall, and Professor Radha Kumar moved a resolution expressing sympathy with him for the loss. The resolution was circulated among the participants for their signatures. The participants including the Pakistani guests endorsed the resolution and signed it.

The president of Kashmir Bar Association Mian Qayum and some other lawyers from the Valley refused to sign the resolution. Radha insisted that it was moved simply because the deceased was related to one of the participants. The conference had an ethical and moral obligation to express sympathy with the bereaved participant. Mian Qayum remained adamant on not signing the resolution. The participants from the separatist camp followed suit and refused to endorse the resolution. I intervened and told Qayum that by not signing the resolution, he was according approval to such killings.

In 2006, Sushobha Barve's Centre for Dialogue and Reconciliation organised a conference in a hotel in Jammu. There was representation of almost every political group in the conference. During the discussion, senior lawyer Zaffar Shah rudely interrupted Nizamuddin Bhat of PDP. Shah vocally argued that mainstream political parties of Kashmir have no right to speak on the Kashmir problem. Shah's unsolicited remarks made me angry. I told him that his remarks were in order if he were the sole proprietor of the Kashmir conflict. The mainstream leaders who were at the conference, I said, had come only for one thing. They wanted an account of the NC, Congress and CPI(M) workers who were killed by you in thousands.

It is extremely sad that the separatists and also the religious clergy in Kashmir approve the killings perpetrated by the militants. They do not find anything wrong with the extrajudicial killings perpetrated by the militants. This thinking has taken root among youngsters across the Valley. Kashmiri youth now celebrate such killings. And prominent lawyers support them!

The Kashmir conflict is a festering wound. It needs resolution and healing.

But the kind of society that we now have in Kashmir is beyond what we bargained for, when we started with the *masla-e-Kashmir* – the Kashmir issue.

I accept that India has committed blunders in Kashmir and continues to do so. It has perpetuated gross human rights violations in Kashmir. Who can deny this? But what about our own people? What about the protesters who destroy property worth crores in a single day to enforce a shutdown?

My brother told me with pride and honour that during the 2016 agitation, he targeted about 500 private vehicles on the national highway passing through Kashmir.

On the Khanabal-Qazigund road in south Kashmir, a pregnant woman undergoing labour pain was being taken to hospital in a car. Protesting youngsters stopped the car and refused to let it pass. The family was told that they would be allowed to go only if the woman showed her abdomen to prove that she was pregnant.

There are hundreds of such incidents that have happened through the length and breadth of Kashmir. These incidents hammer home the point that the Kashmiri youth are now cruel and even monstrous in their approach towards fellow human beings. Why?

This is because the political leaders and religious preachers have made them so. If this is not religious bigotry, religious fundamentalism, then what is it?

This was the third time that the video of a person killed in Shopian district by militants was released on social media. On November 16 last year, a video of 17-year-old Nadeen Manzoor pleading for mercy was released after his body was found in Niklora village in the district. The day after, another video surfaced of an unidentified man slitting the throat of 19-year-old Huzaif Ashraf Kuttay in Hermain village in Shopian. This is Kashmir's story today, filling my K file.

Militant Recruitment continues Unabated

Despite the massive crackdown on militancy, authorities in Kashmir are struggling to stop recruitment in 'new age' insurgency. The seven youth who went missing since 15 January 2019 are believed to have joined militancy.

Police sources have said most of these youngsters are students from the restive south Kashmir's Pulwama, Anantnag and Shopian districts, and central Kashmir's Budgam district. They were reported missing by their families.

In most cases, youth were reported missing either after the killing of their relatives, or they lived near the areas where militants were killed in encounters. They had been in contact with militants.

Police and intelligence agencies have stated in media reports that *it is a trend for overground workers to join militant groups after the militants they worked with are killed in encounters. The new development is a major setback to the efforts of the Jammu and Kashmir government to wean youth from militancy.* A new rehabilitation policy for surrendered militants is likely to be rolled out soon.

This puts a question mark on the claim of the authorities that fresh recruitment in militancy has stopped. Militant funerals, a fertile ground for militant recruitment, continue to attract thousands of people despite curbs and arrests. The year 2018 was the bloodiest in a decade in Kashmir, with security forces gunning down 267militants, most of them local youths. About 160 civilians and 159 armed forces personnel were also killed the same year.

2019 began with four youth from southern Kashmir's Shopian and Pulwama districts missing from their homes. Their families had no information of their sons' whereabouts for more than a week. All four families filed missing person's reports in their respective police stations after failing to establish any contact with the youth despite repeated attempts and searches. Earlier, recruits used to release photographs of their joining and brandished guns. There may be some internal policy now not to release such photographs, since encounters are common now.

Militancy in Kashmir has seen many ups and downs during the last three decades.

This is not because of lack of arms and ammunition imported from the other side. Militancy has continued to survive essentially because of ideological support from radical Islam. 'Operation All Out' was launched with much fanfare and determination, encounters took place on an almost daily basis, and fresh recruitment happened at the same pace.

Those who argue that in Kashmir militants can be flushed out ignore the basic premise. It is not the number of actual recruits into militancy but the indoctrination that keeps militancy alive in Kashmir.

Security forces say there is no option but to kill the militants. In their opinion, *talking* to militants represents a betrayal of fundamental values and principals as it appears to legitimise violence. It promotes discourse with men who have no respect for the law and norms of society. They even argue that if you *talk* to terrorists, you are fulfilling their aim.

Since 2014, the doctrine operational in Kashmir is that 'saving one life endangers hundreds'. In February 2018, a high-profile Pakistani militant escaped from police custody during medical check-up in a Srinagar hospital. With this, the doctrine of elimination got tacit institutional support. According to this philosophy, elimination is actually the first step towards the endgame.

Facts and figures suggest that this doctrine is not working, as the cycle is continuing unabated. As an insider, I would suggest that the 'coercive' policy alone won't work. Rather – it has never worked.

The challenge is not fighting the militants. The challenge lies in handling the militant mindset which has strong ideological foundations.

After the barbaric incident of killing a young woman in Shopian in ISIS style, it becomes even more difficult to draw moral comfort in arguing that one should engage with those who have committed such heinous crimes. Governments usually walk a thin moral line whenever they engage with the terrorists. But in Kashmir, the doctrine must be 'Kill the sin but not sinner'. This again is a moral dilemma. Engagement for what? Does it amount to giving in to demands?

One can achieve the maximum by giving minimum, provided you have the courage.

The courage comes from the in-depth understanding of the causes of violence.

In Kashmir, apologists have over-simplified the case. The conflict and the subsequent mishandling of Kashmir by the

Indian state cannot be ignored or denied. The incumbent Governor of Jammu and Kashmir Satyapal Malik has repeatedly admitted this. Also, one needs political imagination to address the Kashmir issue. I am not going to write about the political dimensions of the conflict. There are tomes written already on the subject.

What I have learnt from conflict studies is that you need a human and holistic approach more than political roadmaps to deal with extremism. In Kashmir, you need to do something nice without actually doing anything. It is your approach that shall determine the success rate. You have to be very careful to avoid creating perverse conditions that shall encourage more violence, rather than help in ending it.

Bottom Line

In the Kashmir conflict, even the separatists who comprise its political leadership, don't know about the endgame. The militants fighting in the countryside may not even know what they are fighting for. But one thing is for sure. The ideology that they pursue has so far not succeeded in making them irreconcilable. True that they represent the Pakistani interest rather than the Kashmiri interest. Hence, they will always insist on talking to Pakistan.

The government can still speak to them and help them understand their aim better. If you make this the bottom-line, you will not be embarrassed even if you fail. Initially, the target group should be unarmed aggressive youth. With them, the chances of success are higher.

What we are aiming at here is the transformation from violence to participation and undercutting the grievances on which it rides.

This is also important, given the current scenario in which armed groups receive significant political support from the most vulnerable section of the society, viz. the youth. If you succeed in making your enemies your friends, you may be able to end the animosity.

It amazes me to observe that the Indian Army visualised this long before the political dispensation could. The mechanism for the same must be taken up by the policy-makers. The success rate will be higher if intermediaries are used for the same. One can deny association with them if required.

Women of Kashmir

THE TRANSFORMATION of Kashmir society from a tolerant and peaceful one to violent extremism has been founded on basic premise of the 'victimhood' narrative. This victimhood rhetoric has four precepts.

One, oppression of Kashmiris by the Indian state.

Two, India kills our people.

Three, Muslims across the globe are a single entity.

Four, kill them as they kill us elsewhere.

I disagree with people who say that the extremist narratives in Kashmir or elsewhere in the Muslim world are driven by a few violent groups, and that the Muslim community is peace-loving. There are some inbuilt and inherent misinterpretations and misrepresentations of Islamic teachings that have gone deep into us.

These misrepresentations have made Muslims across the world think uniquely in terms of 'Us and Them'. Over the last few decades, this thought process has dealt a severe blow to the cultural, civilisational and geographical identities within the Islamic community. The result is that *Muslims across the world have shifted their focus from spirituality to exhibitionist Islam.* Politically, the thought process envisages a single Muslim identity. This fresh rhetoric of Islamic identity has replaced regional and territorial nationalism among the Muslim community. This rhetoric is also at the core of the ideology which seeks to establish the global caliphate.

Kashmiri Muslims too are influenced by this ideology, which was initially imported from Pakistan. It was strengthened in the later decades by Saudi Wahabism. *The uniqueness of this ideology is that it feeds on the same set of grievances all over the Muslim world.*

In Kashmir, the set of grievances has been no different. The grievances against the Indian state were catalytic in the quick spread of this ideology. Killing and attacking 'them' was legitimised. Soon, it was accorded social sanction.

Women in Kashmir are pivotal in constructing these deadly narratives. It is tragic that they are building these narratives in great innocence. They believe it is their religious duty to fight the 'takfir' .

Women are the most vulnerable section of Kashmir's society. They are the real victims of conflict. They are also the main agents for the transformation of the society. Women comprise the largest natural institution which influences the children.

As a keen and close watcher of the events which unfolded in Kashmir over the last few decades, I have seen mothers play a very important role in radicalising their sons without having any idea of its consequences. The 'Us versus Them' narrative constructed by the extremists has invariably influenced mothers in average middle class and poor families. The hate-filled chest is the natural feeder of the child, and the consequences are there for everyone to see.

The romanticisation and glorification of militants, both before and after death, has an immediate impact on the thought processes of an uneducated mother who has no exposure to the outer world. Over the last few years, we saw mothers giving gun salute to their slain militant son at funeral processions. This is a deep psychological mania that is being romanticised. This appeals to the emotionally charged and vulnerable women most dramatically.

This is no secret that the mother of a poster-boy militant commander becomes a potential recruiter after her son is killed. In certain cases, mothers have wished such romantic death for their young sons. *We are living through times when the atmosphere in Kashmir is emotionally charged with mythical and mystical heavenly promises.*

As someone who has been watching this churning closely, I disagree with the terror apologists, and also the many ignorant people in the establishment. Apologists continue to manufacture stories to justify radicalism. The state continues in complete denial mode, as if everything is under control.

The apologists in Kashmir and outside attribute everything to the conflict. They ignore the ramifications of the emerging situation as per their convenience. *Several groups have developed huge vested interest in the status quo in Kashmir. The apologists are among those who thrive on the conflict economy.* For them, this has emerged as a huge industry which needs no physical infrastructure. *Provocation is the only fuel it needs.*

The 'Us versus Them' narrative is being sold to every household in Kashmir. Women, who are at the receiving end of this indoctrination, absorb this poisonous narrative with totality. Anger, hate and negative religious sentiment has successfully penetrated every household. It has deep psychological bearings on the average woman in Kashmir.

Indoctrination of the Mothers

Even though the patriarchal character of Kashmir society enjoys religious legitimacy, the extremist interpretation of Islam has sufficiently converted women to the violent form of extremism. There are hundreds of madrasas established by Jamaat-e-Islami in the Valley exclusively for women. In the early '90s, Hizbul Mujahideen had a women's squad. Women preachers would go from village to village. They would address congregations of women and glorify the participation of women in jihad. There are madrasas for women to impart them higher education, and also inculcate in them the hardcore religious values.

The alleged human rights abuses perpetuated by the security forces, particularly sexual harassment, are aggressively taken up on various online and offline mediums, by women. I am in total agreement that all human rights abuses and sexual harassment cases must be aggressively questioned and challenged. But it is clear that this campaign is taken up with the objective of spreading hate. Such crimes, where the accused are militants or even local Kashmiris, are not similarly questioned.

Such campaigns effectively contribute towards hardening narratives among the women in Kashmir. Violent Islam has contributed greatly to a rigidly entrenched gender hierarchy in Kashmir.

Religion has redefined the identity of women in Kashmir in such a way that the woman can move straightway from the four walls of her house to the battlefield, but she cannot see the world in between.

It has been theorised that there are only three pre-requisites in an adult woman's life. These are home – looking after her husband and children. Hijab – covering herself from head to feet. Hijrat – migration of carrying out holy war and subsequently enjoy eternal life in heaven.

There are madrasas in some areas in Kashmir where the resident girl students have no contact with the outside world for weeks or months together. They cannot visit their parents for months. Nobody can visit them. The only occasion when they are sent home is on the eve of the two Eids. Parents cannot get their daughter home even on the death of a close relative.

On the busy streets in the urban centers of Kashmir, one can see women in hundreds busy in day-to-day life.

There are many truths about Kashmir. The larger truths lie somewhere in the countryside.

Even in urban centers, there are hundreds of madrasas imparting education to girls, but simultaneously intoxicating them to alarming levels. The presence of even one teacher adhering to extremist ideology can influence thousands of raw minds.

In the last three years, Kashmir has seen girls come out of schools and colleges on the slightest provocations to pelt stones on security forces aggressively. The extremist theologists refer to these developments during their Friday sermons with pride and honour. They regard this aggression among women as a great achievement.

Kashmir also has fanatic women's organisations working zealously to indoctrinate women.

This is the only feminist discourse we have in Kashmir. Yes, we discuss atrocities being perpetrated on women by government forces. We even exaggerate and fudge the records to suit our discourse. Women are discussed as a major victim of the conflict. Yes, she certainly is the victim of conflict. But there is no debate around patriarchy or the churning happening worldwide.

There are two major reasons for the transformation of Kashmiri women. One, the Islamisation or religious sanction to the patriarchal character of society, compounded by the deadly conflict of which the woman is the direct victim.

Two, the society is completely a Muslim homogenous society. There is no intermingling of different religious and cultural groups. We have only *azaaan* (call for the faithful) echoing from the minars of mosques all around. The ambience is Islamic. Religion is the most dominant theme occupying the entire social and mental space. Women are preoccupied with passing on the same to the children at home. There is complete obsession with Islam and its teachings. Women are becoming more and more exhibitionist in this dominant discourse. They have authored strict religious diktats for themselves, doing away with the social nuances and practices which were common earlier.

The women are now perhaps the most radicalised section of the Kashmir society. This will have a deep impact on the future discourse. The generation that held tolerant, inclusive and plural social values of the Kashmir society is vanishing fast from the social landscape.

The Older Generation and the Kashmir Conflict

PEOPLE WHO have been involved in Kashmir officially or were part of back-channel talks in the past have an impression that Kashmiris realise that azadi or Pakistan are not the options.

They argue that Kashmiris understand the existing geo-political realities. According to this section, Kashmiris can, therefore, be taken on board provided there is the will to do so. Former RAW Chief AS Dulat and several others still hold the view that Kashmiris are always willing to negotiate. It is the government which lacks the will and courage to talk to the Kashmiris. Most hold the view that it is not difficult to talk to Kashmiris. They believe that Kashmiris have the realisation that azadi or whatever slogans they echo are meaningless.

Their argument is based on their personal experiences on ground zero. Since these people have that vast knowledge and experience, this observation cannot be contested. What they hold is true. The question is – about whom is it true?

I asked Dulat why did he not meet Syed Ali Geelani during all these years in Kashmir. Dulat told me that he was never ever interested in meeting Geelani. He said Geelani was living in some imaginative world far away from this planet. 'My officers meet him regularly. On certain occasions they also suggested that I should meet Geelani, but I was never interested', Dulat told me. I often told Dulat that you should have met Geelani. You have committed a mistake by not meeting him.

The older generation in Kashmir has been realistic and mature enough to understand the nuances of geo-politics. This is the generation about whom Dulat and others talk.

Yes. This generation of Kashmiris is accommodative and forthright. There are many eminent Indians who have tried to address the Kashmir issue with truth and sincerity. They include Dulat, Mani Shankar Aiyar, SK Lamba, Wajahat Habibullah, Swami Agnivesh, Sushoba Barve, Seema Mustsfa, Radha Kumar and many others. The problem is that even the best of them have not observed the perceptional flaws in the approach of the people of their generation in Kashmir.

The older generation of Kashmir, though reasonably moderate and well meaning, has nurtured a unique thought process in their outlook which is flawed and flimsy. They have always looked towards New Delhi and Islamabad. They have not shouldered their own responsibility towards their society. Instead, they have consistently passed on the buck to New Delhi and Islamabad.

Yes, this generation has presented itself as the principal party to the dispute or the main stakeholders. But their actions have not matched their words. This unique thought process has crept deep into the subconscious of the average Kashmiri of that age group. I have personally witnessed Kashmiris blaming New Delhi and Islamabad for family disputes.

In 2013, the daughter of a close relative of mine was married to the son of a Jamaati. The relationship suffered a blow when the young man came under the radar of security agencies for having contacts with militants. The bride left her husband's house and came back to her parents'. When I heard that the young woman was back, I called up her father to enquire why the relationship was not working. Instead of giving me the account, he abruptly started cursing India and Pakistan.

Kashmiris of the older generation have always looked towards New Delhi and have never owned up their responsibility towards building a peaceful Kashmir.

They are stakeholders, but they have never acted as stakeholders. All their talk centers around Delhi should do this, Delhi should do that. Delhi should take this step, Delhi should take that step. This is their mantra for the future of their society. Talking to Kashmiris of this generation is futile.

The leaders of the 'movement' have lost the status of being the stakeholders for all practical purposes. Why? One, *they don't enjoy any kind of influence on the younger generation anymore.* Second, they cannot move an inch without instructions from Pakistan. Third, *they do not have the courage to suggest a roadmap.*

This is precisely what LK Advani, when he was Deputy Prime Minister, said about the Hurriyat leaders who met him at least twice officially. *They were told by Advani to come up with the roadmap for the resolution of the Kashmir dispute. This never happened.* The peaceniks sitting in Delhi could not highlight this travesty.

Of course, the older generation of Kashmiris is moderate.

But the problem with them is that they will never do anything that would invite the wrath of Pakistan or even the furious younger generation in Kashmir. They will always say that Delhi must do something.

Even if Delhi does anything positive tomorrow, would they be able to sell it? I am afraid not. The existing extremist Islamic narrative has further aggravated the problem for the separatist leadership. Only Geelani is left unscathed by the anger that now subsumes the young generation of the Kashmiris towards the separatist leaders.

Yasin Malik, who was the only hope for the secularist and moderates in Kashmir, has been compelled to redefine himself under the emerging scenario. He is no more a liberal or a Gandhian, as he appeared to be earlier. He is now a hardcore Islamist at least in his posturing.

The Government of India has to be blamed equally for the present mess where the moderates are no longer moderate. Kashmiris are well-acquainted with the policy of the Government of India in Kashmir. They call it the 'use and throw policy'. *The Indian government never allowed the moderate constituency in Kashmir to grow and strengthen.* The result is before us. It is the Government of India which squeezed the space for moderates in Kashmir.

The older generation in Kashmir, right from the common man to the separatists, suffers from a perceptional syndrome where the younger Kashmiris are concerned. The older generation is consistently crying that they have no say anymore in the society. The furious, indoctrinated younger generation has taken control of everything from the home to the mosque.

But whose fault is this? The older generation romanticised militancy, suicidal ideology and this attitude of rejection. They conveniently allowed the younger generation to destroy societal values and norms. They conditioned them to be radicals.

The teenagers ruling the streets, killing and getting killed for three decades, were mostly from the weaker sections of the society. Now they have taken over completely. The damage has been done. The only person who has gained from the mob mentality ruling Kashmir is Syed Ali Geelani. From Day One, he encouraged this mentality ideologically and practically at ground level.

The argument that Kashmiris are mature enough to understand the nuances of geopolitics and that we can have a deal with them is outdated. It has lost the context in new-age Kashmir 2020. The reality is altogether different. Of course, this thought was relevant at one point of time. But today, the argument has lost all relevance in Kashmir.

The terrorist attack on the CRPF convoy on 14 February at Lethpora by a Kashmiri suicide bomber is an indicator of how bad the situation in Kashmir is, and where Kashmir is headed. But Kashmiris in their 50s and 60s still look towards New Delhi and Islamabad for mitigating their sufferings.

Tragically, *people in Delhi choose to address this age group alone. This makes their understanding flawed.* The strength of the active militant groups JeM, LeT, HM and others cannot be measured through the number of active militants on ground. Their strength lies in the ideological leanings of the younger generation in Kashmir, who far outnumber the people striving for peace.

It is in this context that I suggest that the conventional wisdom of talking to political leaders is no longer relevant. The Government of India must reach out to militant groups through channels which are immune to breakdowns.

The leaders of these militant groups are sitting across the fence. There are many poster boys on our side. The communication channel should have access to both sides of the LoC. It is in this backdrop that I suggest that *the Government of India should hire a neutral person from outside to do the job.* This way, the government will not dilute its policy of not talking to terrorists. And yet, the talk will happen. The important thing is that the government can deny it when required.

Run-up to the Present

ON 30 March 2019, I was in Hyderabad when I heard the news. Yet another Kashmiri militant had tried to blow up his explosives-laden vehicle and strike the CRPF convoy at Banihal on the Srinagar-Jammu National Highway. I was not surprised. I anticipate more such attacks in the near future. I believe Kashmiri militants will try to repeat the Pulwama attack as and when they get the opportunity to strike.

I will not attribute this to the failure of the security agencies, as is being done by most stakeholders. Kashmiri militants need only expertise from Pakistan for the preparation of explosives. Suicide bombers are available locally.

The new breed of militants in Kashmir can be encapsulated in the expression 'dead men walking'. They love death like we love life. The failed attack on the CRPF at Banihal came

45 days after the 14 February suicide bombing on a CRPF convoy at Lethpora near Pulwama, in which 45 paramilitary personnel were killed. Fortunately, in March, the suicide bomber did not succeed in triggering the blast in Banihal. A tragedy was averted.

The harsh fact is that another Kashmiri militant was so soon ready to blow himself up to inflict mortal wounds on the Indian security agencies.

The question we face is this: What motivates Kashmiri militants to become suicide bombers? Is it the perceived set of grievances against the state? Or *is there* something more than meets the eye?

I have consistently argued over the last few years that the current phase of violence in Kashmir is beyond the political narratives of azadi and self-determination. It is time to acknowledge this truth.

Apologists both within and outside Kashmir are trying to portray the movement as violent resistance to state oppression. I don't buy this argument. The atmospherics we have in Kashmir points towards a far grave problem than we perceive.

The current militancy in Kashmir has reached an advanced stage, courtesy the ideological upbringing of the younger generation. The so-called political conflict and the 'dispute' still remain centre-stage, but the issue is far more complicated. We have a whole generation of indoctrinated youngsters who have gone crazy, and are yearning to embrace death 'in the glory of Islam'.

Given the historical perspective, we tend to take positions on Kashmir based on old narratives. We tend to discuss Kashmir based on our knowledge or understanding of the historical perspective. I find this the greatest error in understanding the

Kashmir conundrum.

The present phase of violence in Kashmir has very little to do with the nature of conflict that history threw before us. This understanding, rather misunderstanding of the issue, exonerates the stakeholders from many crucial responsibilities. Of course, the political problem of Kashmir and its dimensions are intact, at least for the sake of argument. The stakeholders now hide behind what we have known as the 'political conflict'. Thinkers and opinion leaders continue to invoke Kashmir in the political and historical context nationally and internationally. A significant section of the Indian intelligentsia and people in international community also side with thus argument. The stakeholders are engaged in the blame game, while the problem we face currently is far more grievous.

The narrative, however, has changed dramatically though no one wants to admit it.

The Kashmir intelligentsia including opinion leaders, journalists, academics and writers are today telling us that this is a war of civilisations. There is agreement among them that Kashmir is a *separate nation*, not a separate political entity. Most Kashmiri thinkers argue on the same lines. We heard some Kashmiris dominant in the separatist and militancy circles declare lately that *Kashmir is not a political issue, it is a religious issue.* The fresh extremist narrative is of war between Dar-al-Islam (House of Islam) and Dar-al-harab (House of war, countries not under Islamic rule).

This intellectualisation of the Kashmir issue has left unattended the transformation and churning which Kashmir has undergone in the recent years.

In the current phase of Kashmir violence, the narrative is not driven by political and social scientists. It is driven by the religious leaders and preachers. Azadi does not have the potential to transform a whole generation of youth. It is the Islamist ideology that is producing the dead men walking in Kashmir who love and seek death the way others love and seek life.

This is peculiar with Muslim societies across the world, which allowed Islamist Salafis (Wahabis) and Jamaat-e-Islami to flourish in their lands. Kashmir is witnessing the second wave of proselytisation after Kashmiri Pandits converted to Islam in days Sufism first settled in Kashmir many centuries ago. Modern is the conversion from mainstream (Sufi) Islam to the Islam peddled by Jamaat- e-Islami, founded by Maududi in 1941. The reason for the conversion is that the theologians and scholars of mainstream Islam failed to articulate the genuine theology of the religion. Their failure pushed Kashmiri Muslims towards radicalised Islam. The result is for everyone to witness.

From 2002 to 2006

To compound the problem, extremist Islamist ideologies were allowed unbridled expansion by political leaders as part of the pact between power-politics and religion. This was most visible in the period from 2002 to 2006. As chief minister of Jammu and Kashmir, Mufti Mohammad Sayeed allowed extremist Islamists to reorganise and strengthen themselves. He encouraged them in doing so. The secret pact between PDP and Jamaat-e-Islami was no secret in Kashmir. The Indian deep state was aware of it.

The Indian deep state has documented accounts which reveal the nexus between Mufti and the Jamaatis dating back to 1971-72.

The Jamaat helped Mufti in defeating the National Conference in 2002. Mufti ascended as chief minister and rewarded the Jamaat with complete freedom. Jamaat's ideology of hate and the 'us versus them' doctrine flourished under Mufti. This is not an isolated period of their nexus, it is decades old.

The apologists are doing a great disservice by hiding behind narratives of 'rights and responsibilities'. Both Jamaat-e-Islami and Salafis have consensually and conveniently made it a war between the believers of Islam and non-believers. This doctrine provides human resource to the current phase of violence in Kashmir. This pop-Islamism derived from Maududi's literature is totally in contravention to the mainstream, true Islam.

Pakistan is facing severe terrorism, though it does not have any Kashmir issue. Terrorism has killed thousands of Pakistanis even though it is an independent, self-ruled country.

Let us presume that India, Pakistan and the Kashmiri people tomorrow resolve the so-called political issue of Kashmir.

Will it lead to normalcy in Kashmir? No.

The kind of transformation that has happened in Kashmir will not allow our society to live peacefully. The US, in a deal with the Al Qaeda, has handed over Afghanistan to the Taliban in 2020 and the Taliban want to be friends with India. Do we expect that Afghanistan will be peaceful now? No.

The theology that glorifies death and condemns life is here to stay. It will manufacture a new set of grievances to continue with the bloodbath. This is true for Afghanistan. It is true for Kashmir.

Kashmir is in grip of a theology which celebrates death. It is here to stay even if the state honestly and sincerely addresses the present set of grievances. Such a mindset is produced by deep radicalisation. It ritualises violent responses to grievances based on real or perceived social exclusion.

Kashmir does not recognise that social challenges are part of every human society. Alienation, exclusion, discrimination, deprivation, abuse, excesses, torture, denial of rights and so on. What makes Kashmir peculiar is its response to the challenges.

Those ideologically close to leftists, rightists or any cult are known to respond to situations violently. But such responses do not take the shape of group-thinking. Such responses are usually individual or personal. Of late, we are witnessing violent responses of white supremacists.

Violent responses are now in the realm of group-thinking in Muslim-majority societies courtesy the unrealistic, illegitimate interpretation of Islamic teachings by Wahabis and Jamaat-e-Islami. Muslims influenced by this theology respond to grievances violently. Such is their collective response. Some may respond by actively engaging in violence. Others may provide ideological, rather theological inputs. The larger group which does not engage directly in violence provides logistics to the violent members. The larger group, indoctrinated by an illegitimate Islamist theology, celebrates the death of 'others'. Why?

Because extremist religious groups are fundamentally exclusivists. They seek an ethnically 'pure society' as the first step towards 'redemption'.

In the second step, they build the concept of a state that is puritanical. This is how violent theology sustains. If you address the given set of grievances, they manufacture another set to keep the ball rolling. This resolve and resilience derived from extremist theology gradually influences the fence-sitters.

Two things immediately come into play. One, the stakeholders develop huge vested interests. Second, those in the circle of this ideology are not allowed to assess or question it.

Both things are at play in Kashmir today. The elites within the system who have huge vested interests in the conflict are conveniently pushing the younger generation into the battlefield. A sizeable section of the elites are thriving on the conflict economy. They have presence everywhere. They are in politics, in the levers of administration, in the media – everywhere.

Mehbooba Mufti, the former chief minister of Jammu and Kashmir, can now be heard invoking Muslim identity in her speeches everywhere. She was on the forefront on agitating against the ban on Jamaat-e-Islami. Kashmiris in the media and the business community also agitated regarding the ban.

This churning and transformation in Kashmir has alienated mainstream Sufi Islam. Real Islam is not mainstream in Kashmir now. The fringe has replaced it. A peaceful Kashmir and the peace-loving Kashmiri is an irritant for them. They see to it that the one who disagrees is discredited and physically harmed. Dissent is the first causality in extremism. There is a whole generation of elderly Kashmiris who do not subscribe to these deadly extremist narratives. They are mute because they fear for their life.

It is also disturbing to observe that the majority of Kashmiri Muslims have either lost the faculty to critically assess, or they choose not to exercise it.

There is no concrete movement within the society that it should revisit the idea of achieving the desired result through violence. Violence is justified, not condemned. The security forces are condemned in abundance. Rizwan Assad's death in police custody infuriated the whole Valley. People took to streets to protest against the police. Strike calls were given by the separatists and also by trade bodies. Businesses and educational institution were shut. On the same day, an 11-year-old boy, Atif, was held captive by militants in north Kashmir for two days. He was finally killed. There was no one to condemn or mourn his death. A couple of terror apologist journalists blamed the security forces for not allowing the militants to escape, so that Atif could be saved.

Such truths emerging from Kashmir horrify non-Muslims, who then become explicit opponents of Islam. They tend to make it an issue of Muslims versus non-Muslims. Kashmiri students and traders had to face abuse in the mainland in the aftermath of the Pulwama terror attack. The abuse they faced made the Kashmir violence seem reactionary – which it is not.

It is essentially Islamist extremism that plays in Kashmir's streets. It sustains on many factors. The brute religious response is an important factor that justifies it.

What Sets it Apart

The current phase of militancy in Kashmir has a very strong ideological basis. It is completely different from what it was in the early 1990s. Islamist theology originating from Wahabism and Maududism provides the requisite ideological input to the current phase of militancy. In that sense it is not different from global jihadist movements. The ideological derivatives are same.

What sets it apart from global jihadism is that militants operating in Kashmir are not organisationally or structurally associated with the Islamist global jihadists. They are still controlled by the Pakistan deep state.

Barring one small group of Ansar Gazwatul Hind once led by the dreaded Zakir Musa, considered to be affiliated to Al Qaeda, all other militant groups in Kashmir are in direct control of the Pakistan deep state. Their ideological foundations, however, are as deadly as that of any other global jihadi organisation. Kashmiri militants are now as much trained for carrying out suicidal attacks as any other Islamist jihadi of foreign origin.

The Pulwama attack of 14 February and the unsuccessful Banihal attack in March were carried out by Kashmiri militants. *Intelligence inputs suggest that there are many more Kashmiri militants who have been trained to carry out suicidal attacks.* This makes the current phase of militancy in Kashmir more deadly in comparison to its early phase.

The militants in Kashmir, across the spectrum of their group affiliation, are playing a strategic numbers game in the Valley. Since 2010, it has been observed that the terrorist organisations operating in Kashmir keep the number of total active militants in the field between 200 and 250. Intelligence officials say that this seems to be a well thought-out tactic on their part.

Vigil on the Line of Control (LoC) and the international border has been stepped up by India in the last few years, making infiltration difficult. At this stage, infiltration on the international border is less about militants crossing over to this side. The higher incidence is of delivery of weapons from the other side.

The Magic Number

The current breed of militants in Kashmir do not require motivational inputs from across the border. The extremist and deadly Islamist ideology has made them hardcore in their approach to violence. This current breed needs only expertise and weapons to sustain. Smuggling weapons from across the border is their major challenge. This is why the militant groups engaged in Kashmir deliberately keep the numbers between 200 and 250.

In 2010, security forces killed about 270 militants in various operations. The number of active militants at the end of that year was around 230. In 2017, around 200 militants were killed by the security forces. At the end of the year, the number of active militants operating in Kashmir was again close to 250. Likewise in 2018, about 260 militants were killed. The number of militants active at the end of 2018 was again around 250. This pattern is being observed for close to a decade.

There is also the issue of finances.

Post 2015, the hawala channels have been largely blocked, and the influx is relatively low. In the sting operation conducted by *India Today* in 2017, senior separatist leader Nayeem Khan admitted that approximately Rs 450 crore were spent to sustain the 2016 agitation. According to estimates, earlier Rs 300 crore was pumped into Kashmir annually through hawala transactions from Pakistan and Arab countries. This money reached separatist leaders, some Trusts and NGOs in fixed sums. The recent crackdowns by the National Investigating Agency succeeded in blocking the influx of hawala money to Kashmir to a considerable extent. The hawala transactions came down drastically following the crackdown on separatists and others involved in the business.

But two channels remain intact. *One is the money coming from Saudi Arabia to build Wahabi infrastructure in Kashmir. According to the police and security agencies, Saudi money flows unhindered in Kashmir.*

The second is the annual outlay of the Pakistan deep state for Kashmir. According to intelligence sources, this amount is between Rs 150-200 crore. Out of this, Rs 50 crore approximately is provided to organisations like Jaish-e-Muhammad (JeM) and Lashkar-e-Taiba (LeT) to facilitate the smuggling of weapons from Pakistan, and also the infiltration of militants. Rs 100 to 150 crore are provided for the logistics of the militants operating in Kashmir. Senior police officers say the Indian intelligence agencies have provided these figures after getting credible inputs from across the border.

Despite the provision of these large sums, it is argued that enough funds are now not available to the militants and separatists in Kashmir to mobilise big crowds or organise huge protests. From 2014 to 2017, militants have desperately resorted to loot and arson to meet their financial requirements. In several bank dacoities during this period, militants decamped with crores of rupees.

In the Current Phase

In the current phase of Kashmir militancy, the local Kashmiri youth are more inclined towards JeM and LeT when compared to Hizbul Mujahideen, which was earlier regarded as the largest indigenous group. From the perspective of radical Kashmiri youth, there is logic in joining the ranks of JeM or LeT. The Ideological churning of Kashmiri youth makes them identify more with JeM and LeT, which operate from Pakistan and have global jihadist foundations. Currently, about 60 JeM militants are operating in Kashmir. An equal number of Jaish militants have been neutralised since September 2018.

In December 2018, 13 JeM militants infiltrated from Pakistan. JeM militants infiltrate mostly by crossing the international border in the Jammu region. After the Pulwama attack, the security agencies initially were of the opinion that the attack was planned and executed by JeM militants from Kakapora in Pulwama district. Kakapora is about eight kilometers from Lethpora, also in Pulwama district, where the suicide bomber blew up the car loaded with explosives.

But as the investigations proceeded, *security agencies*

were surprised to know that the planning and execution for the Pulwama attack was done at Marhama village in Anantnag district. Marhama is the highest-populated village in Anantnag district. It boasts of five madrasas, belonging to all the five sects of Islam present in Kashmir: Wahabism, Jamaat-e-Islami, Deobandi, Barelvi and Tabhleegi.

Security agencies say Marhama is the new epicenter of Jaish-e-Muhammad. Jaish has a significant presence also in Tral in Pulwama district. Tral houses Madrasa-e-Noor, an old established madrasa run by one Moulvi Noor Ahmad. According to Jammu and Kashmir Police, 70 per cent of the youth who joined militant ranks from Tral were former students of Madrasa-e-Noor.

In Shopian district, Imaam Sahib, Harmain and Zainapora areas have a significant number of Jaish recruits. This area houses one of the biggest Deobandi madrasas of Kashmir Valley. In north Kashmir, Jaish is active with local support in Dangiwacha area of Sopore.

According to security agencies, LeT has about 50 militants active in Kashmir. Out of these, 30 are local while 20 are foreigners, mostly from Pakistan. Extremist religious groups provide theological and human resource support to militant organisations active in Kashmir. The problem is not restricted to armed militants alone.

Security agencies in Kashmir are facing a bigger and more dangerous challenge from unarmed non-combatant youth who are completely radicalised, and are ready to join militant ranks. Security agencies and the police accept that the number of militants active at a time would have been much higher if the militant groups had access to more guns and ammunition. As this has been contained, the Magic Number vacillates between

200 and 300. How to contain this constantly replenishing human resource is the question?

How events unfold in a conflict zone like Kashmir can be understood from the fact that post 14 February Pulwama attack, the Government of India banned the controversial religious extremist organisation Jamaat-e-Islami Jammu and Kashmir for five years because of its nexus with terror outfits. The decision comes a few days after Centre's massive crackdown on its leaders. The five-year ban on the group has been imposed with immediate effect and will be subject to scrutiny of a tribunal constituted by the Ministry of Home Affairs (MHA). Jammu and Kashmir Police arrested over 100 cadres including its chief Abdul Hamid Fayaz and advocate Zahid Ali (spokesperson). The group's leaders are indulging in activities intended to disrupt the territorial integrity of India, New Delhi said.

The decision was taken at a high-level meeting presided over by PM Narendra Modi on 28 February. A notification issued by MHA said that government has imposed a ban on the group under the Unlawful Activities (Prevention) Act.It said that Jamaat-e-Islami Jammu and Kashmir was in close touch with militant groups and was looking to escalate secessionist movement in the border State.

In the past, there have been allegations that Jamaat-e-Islami Jammu and Kashmir is the political arm of the banned terror outfit Hizbul Mujahideen. The Kashmir chapter of the Jamaat was founded in 1945 as a chapter of the Jamaat-e-Islami Hind and separated in 1953 due to differences over political ideology. It was first banned in 1990 but this ban lapsed in 1995. However, the Jamaat reinforced itself on the political landscape only in the year 2001, after reaching a pact with the then establishment in New Delhi, under Vajpayee-Advani rule.

Though there are conflicting reports about the pact, one thing which was more than evident after 2001 is that Jamaat shifted from striving for establishment of the Islamic state through jihad to socio-religious activities. Dulat said, Bhat was very keen to save the carders of Jamaat and he, with the support of other senior leaders of the organisation, had decided to dissociate the Jamaat from the Hizbul mujahideen. But, others told me, the arrangement was not as simple as it appeared to be. A senior intelligence officer on the request of anonymity told me that the understanding was based on the assurance of Jamaat Chief GM Bhat that the revival of his organisation would be *based on the premise of condemning violence in all its forms and manifestations.* He said that Bhat had also assured New Delhi that it would be a different Jamaat-e-Islami which would not only dissociate from the violence but would condemn it unequivocally. The intelligence officer also said that Bhat also committed to bring the Jamaat in the mainstream gradually.

The agreement was followed by the parties in letter and spirit at the beginning. The hardliner hawkish Syed Ali Geelani was expelled from the Jamaat and the carders were strictly directed not to associate with the narrative of separatism and jihadism individually or collectively.

But the dichotomy was that Jamaat continued to receive money from Pakistan through hawala channels for what it called *charitable* or *philanthropic* activities. Soon Bhat was succeeded by Ghulam Hasan Sheikh as Ameer-e-Jamaat. Bhat was again shifted to Falah-e-Aam trust. Jamaat was receiving money from Pakistan in the name of the trust owned by it. The transaction was made through the Pak-based Jamaat leader Sona Ullah Dar who had crossed over to that side in early nineties. The money flowed in bulk and Jamaat slowly, but steadily shifted back to its core ideology of establishing a Caliphate.

Soon Ghulam Hasan Sheikh was succeeded by Muhammad Abdullah Wani. Both would, however, officially maintain that Jamaat believes in peaceful resolution of Kashmir problem through dialogue. Both would still avoid invoking jihad and UN Resolutions publicly. However, things changed dramatically when Bhat was again reelected as Ameer-e-Jamaat in 2015. Reportedly Bhat wanted to remove Sona Ullah Dar as the hawala channel. Dar was deeply disturbed by Bhat's move and he leveled the charges of embezzlement of hawala money against Bhat. The issue snowballed and Bhat lost control over the organisation. As a result, the younger generation – in violation of the terms of agreement reached between the establishment and Jamaat in 2001 – started preaching jihad in mosques and religious congregation across the State. Bhat was discredited for his alleged links with the Indian deep state.

In September 2018 the hardliner hawkish Hamid Fayaz was elected Ameer-e-Jamaat and Bhat was voted out. Soon the Jamaat carders started openly embracing jihad and establishment of the Caliphate. Rejuvenated carders of Jamaat soon dominated the narrative in Kashmir.

After the ban imposed on it on 28 February, Jamaat's political arm PDP hit the streets and demanded revocation of ban. Mehbooba got an issue in hand to reassert herself. The elections to the Lok Sabha were around the corner and Jamaat got support from almost every political party in Kashmir.

Mehbooba Mufti, former chief minister of Jammu and Kashmir described the ban on Jamaat 'as interference in religion'. This statement clearly substantiates my argument about the existence of a special secret bond between Mehbooba and

Jamaat-e-Islami. Mehbooba is simply following the footprints of her late father Mufti Mohammad Sayeed in using the Jamaat-e-Islami platform against National Conference. There are strong evidences which suggest that in the 1970s, Sayed Mir Qasim, the then chief minister and Mufti Mohammad Sayeed used the mullahs of Jamaat-e-Islami against Sheikh Muhammad Abdullah.

History bears testimony to the fact that Qasim and Mufti provided Jamaat leaders, mostly the mullahs, government properties to hold congregations against Sheikh. The Lala Rukh Hotel and Budshah hotel (the Tourism Development Corporation properties) at the city centre Lal Chowk were being provided to Jamaat free to propagate extremist version of Islam. Its fire brand orator Syed Ali Geelani used these venues for aggressive Sheikh bashing. The Jamaat platform was used specifically against Sheikh. Qasim and Mufti would facilitate events of theJamaat. A senior civil society member from Srinagar's down town area, Ghulam Muhammad Bhat told this writer that he was part of many such congregations of Jamaat held in Lala Rukh and Budshah hotels owned by the Tourism Development Corporation. The congregations were facilitated by Mir Qasim and Mufti Sayeed. One of the founding members of PDP, Ghulam Hasan Mir makes an honest admission about the role of Jamaat in the formation of PDP. Mir said that Mufti would hold separate secret meetings with the Jamaat carders at his Nawgam residence from 1999 to 2002.

Even today, when the Jamaat has been banned and its leaders booked under law, PDP leaders, in an attempt to create a space for themselves, went in support of the jihad ideology. A statement from a PDP leader from Tral, the hotbed of militancy, is reproduced here to prove how far PDP can go to defend and nurse the extremist ideology in Kashmir. A local News gathering agency, KNS reports, 'People's Democratic Party leader and former MLA of Tral, Mushtaq Ahmed Shah lambasted National Conference President Farooq Abdullah for calling Burhan Wani a terrorist'.

'Calling Burhan Wani a terrorist is spiteful and insulting to say the very least. Farooq Abdullah's statement has once again unveiled the real ideology of NC and proved it a party of shameless killers', Shah said in a statement.

Shah added that Farooq Abdullah should know that it was his son Omar Abdullah's government that forced Burhan Wani to take up the gun after being humiliated and tortured along with his brother by forces under Omar's watch.Farooq Abdullah should realise that it was the sheer magnitude of despotism that forced an entire generation to take up arms against deceit and disempowerment perpetrated by NC, Shah said.

Shah added, youth of Kashmir have rendered countless sacrifices to seek political solution to the Kashmir problem and Farooq Abdullah calling an entire generation as terrorists is shameless and a brazen attempt to please his friends in Delhi, the agency reported. 'From pledging to lay foundation stone of Ram mandir at Ayodhya to calling Burhan a terrorist, Farooq Abdullah would go to any extent to please his masters in Delhi for his lust of power', Shah said.

'Institution of sacrifices in Kashmir is sacred and Abdullah should at least leave it out of his petty politics', Shah said, reports the KNS agency.

Engineer Rashid, former law maker, also carried out a protest in Lal Chowk area in Srinagar city demanding lifting of ban on Jamaat. To that extent it was okay as everyone in a democratic country is free to express his views. What was, however, interesting was the kind of slogans Rashid resorted to during his protest march. He raised slogans like: '*Hum sab Jamaati hein* (we all are jamaatis).' This actually reflects the situation on the ground in Indian Kashmir – which means that Jamaat ideology is now mainstream Islam in Kashmir and it has replaced the old traditional tolerant Sufi Islam in Kashmir.

This was also evident from the kind of protests observed by students in Kashmir University. *Greater Kashmir* in its news report dated 13 March 2019 wrote, and I quote: 'Kashmir University students on Wednesday staged a protest against the ban on Jama'at-e-Islami and alleged harassment of their mates by the varsity administration. Scores of students boycotted their classes and staged a demonstration inside the varsity. The protesting students were demanding release of all Jama'at members who have been arrested during the past few weeks across the State. They also accused the varsity administration of selective "harassment" of the students without any "sound reasons". "The varsity authorities have prepared a list of more than two dozen students who are harassed on one pretext or the other", said a protesting student. The students were carrying banners with messages like "ban on Jama'at is a ban on Islam."'

Kashmir Chamber of Commerce, Kashmir Economic Alliance and other trade bodies also held protests against banning Jamaat-e-islami. Social media was flooded by the condemnations and demands for revocation of ban against Jamaat. The same people and forums keep condemning the right-wing RSS for spreading hate against the Muslims and demand ban on right Hindu organisations. Back home, they defend Jamaat – which beyond any doubt promotes exclusivism and extremism. Interestingly, the argument put forward by everyone individually and collectively in support of their demand of lifting ban on Jamaat is that the organisation has been engaged in huge charitable activities. And the Hindutva apologists on the mainland also argue in a similar manner about the RSS, saying that the organisation is the largest in India involved in charity and social upliftment.

The point I am trying to make is that the warped assortment of theology constructed by Maududi's interpretation of Islam has found acceptance among the younger generation in Kashmir to levels beyond imagination.

And the political and business class thriving on the conflict economy do identify with Jamaat to keep themselves relevant to the times. The morally outraged youth have been encouraged by many quarters, particularly the elitist mullahs of non-Kashmiri origin to engage with this theology to safeguard their vested interests. Taking clue from Jamaat, the Wahabi and Deobandi hate preachers too operate in Kashmir through educational charities.

Jamaat has a huge network of educational charities, correlated with the rise of militancy in Kashmir.

The theology constructed by illegitimate interpretation of Islam was initially tolerated by Kashmiri society on the premise that it could not harm the foundations of the society. However, the Jamaat carders who were disciplined to build organisational network on this theology soon challenged the traditional socio-political order of the society and the concept of Islamic jurisprudence was demolished by the activists of Jamaat – leaving the majority of the Muslim population clueless about how to counter this illegitimate theology.

Kashmir's society could not fight the Jamaat theology from the position of strength because of the fact that Pakistan was supporting the Jamaat. Today, in every household, we find one or the other person influenced by Jamaat theology. The dilemma is that Jamaat has a strong support from Pakistan while at the same time it flourishes in Kashmir with the help of mainstream mullahs. There is also a strong intellectual input to this theology which presents it as the mainstream Islam, not as the fringe. The kind of reaction we witnessed to its ban in Kashmir substantiates the argument that the Jamaat theology is now the mainstream islam in Kashmir while Sufi traditional Islam is peripheral.

The mainstream genuine Islamic theology finds it difficult to re-assert in the changing scenario for two reasons. One, it has no godfathers who promote it with conviction, zeal and dedication. All educational institutions in Kashmir, instead of introducing the mainstream theology to the younger generation, propagate Jihadi Islam. Sufi Islam is confined to the older generation which, in any case, has lost relevance in the current extremist narratives.

Secondly, the mainstream theologians fail to provide answers to the problems confronting the society. So, the deviant illegitimate Jamaat theology is expanding without any stiff resistance. The political and other stakeholders in the conflict take full advantage of this vacuum to radicalise society for their own vested interests. Finally, my point is that banning Jamaat-e-islami is no answer to the bigger issue of 'radicalised mindset'. *You need to have legitimate mainstream theologians supported by the institutions to spread the message of love from the position of strength.* They should not be cowed down by the propaganda of the extremists. This should be a force drawing inner strength from the spiritual beauty of the traditional mainstream Islam.

Some Ideas for Change

KASHMIR HAS been a subject of huge interest for scholars across Europe and Asia, essentially because it is a conflict-ridden region.

Of course, it has also been seat of mysticism and learning. But since the conflict started, a sea of literature has been written on Kashmir in the context of conflict. Scholars and observers have closely studied it to examine the areas of conflict management, transformation and resolution. As an insider, I would like to put forth some concrete suggestions for change, keeping in mind the 21st century reality. I am not claiming any expertise on the subject. This is purely a layman's perspective, what I call common sense.

In 2008, under Congress rule, communication channels between Kashmir and New Delhi broke down. For the last 13 years, the demand for dialogue has been constant and persistent from various sections within and outside Kashmir. As the scale of violence intensifies, the demand for dialogue between India and Pakistan, and Srinagar and New Delhi gains momentum.

The current regime is content with the so-called muscular policy. Since the beginning of 2018, observers and also insiders in the government suggested that there were remote chances of any kind of engagement because of the elections scheduled in the first half of 2019. Suggesting or expecting anything like a dialogue at this stage would have seemed childish. *But sooner or later, there has to be engagement with Kashmir*, notwithstanding who the next prime minister is or will be. National elections have come and gone and Prime Minister Narendra Modi is on a second term, batting on a stronger wicket than in the last five years. *A nation which is secular and democratic in its outlook cannot afford to be in denial mode all the time.* This realisation is seen among the hawkish sections of the present regime too.

It is unfortunate that India is constantly in election mode. The incumbent prime minister never came out of election gear during his five-year term. In my interactions with diverse individuals in Delhi after the 2014 election, I would constantly hear that after the assembly elections in this State or that, things will change in Kashmir. This cycle continued for five years. Every time it was said that the government may think, rather was thinking about doing something after 'these election'. In a democracy as large as India, these elections can never end.

Walk with the Devil, Talk, Talk and Talk

The problem with electoral democracy is that you are always looking for electoral benefits at the cost of long-term policy issues.

There is no option but to talk. I attach least significance to the rhetorical statement often repeated by the Indian government that terror and talks cannot go together. I suggest what John F Kennedy said, 'Let us never negotiate out of fear. But let us never fear to negotiate'. President Franklin D Roosevelt, while aligning with Stalin during World War II, justified it by saying, 'It is permitted you in times of grave danger to walk with the devil until you have crossed the bridge'.

This should be the guiding principal for both the contending forces to *defuse* the situation. I am consciously choosing the words because I want to avoid the oft-beaten phraseology of 'resolution'. The study of negotiations in conflict zones across the globe shows that the first step towards the building of dialogue is the *restoration of confidence to talk*, immaterial of whether you are talking from the position of strength or you have lost bargaining power.

What does this imply?

It means – conflict essentially arises out of lack of confidence.

How to restore confidence which can encourage and which can help the parties in conflict to come to the negotiating table? In 2010, the then Home Minister P Chidambaram, told Parliament that Kashmir had acceded to India in unique circumstances. Hence it needed a unique approach. Let me build my first suggestion on this premise.

I strongly believe that you need some *uniqueness* to bring the Kashmiris to the table. It is very important that Kashmiris have confidence in the process of dialogue. Let us approach it in a unique way. I enlist certain measures which could help restore some semblance of order in society. The political initiatives that are needed have been discussed many times over.

I have discussed at length the problems faced by Kashmir

society as a consequence of the violent turmoil. I will restrict myself only to this aspect of the Kashmir imbroglio.

Let us take an overview of the present violent phase in Kashmir before we discuss the remedial measures. We are aware that youth in Kashmir have moved towards the radicalised form of Islam. This is my thesis. There has been a distinct shift to new social setting based on allegiance to a particular group. The more that young Muslims are isolated from the wider social strata, the more vulnerable they are to extremist ideologies.

In this Himalayan region, *we have failed to acknowledge that we have accorded religious sanction to extremist ideology instead of denouncing it as profoundly wrong.*

We have not accepted the theory that the state's over-militarised response is fueling extremism in Kashmir. Violation of human rights by security forces has constantly given a new lease of life to violent ideologies. Violence in Kashmir sustains on atrocities committed by government agencies.

Misgovernance is also a huge factor contributing to insurgency in Kashmir. *Corruption and nepotism has consistently pushed the youth to the utopian vision of a state that is governed by religious laws and is perfect.* This vision has made them choose extremist ideologies to realise such a state. But they do not want such a Kashmir; they are fighting for a Caliphate for the world, located in Kashmir.

It is a fact that extremist Islamist ideology, which is considered the gateway to jihadism, is here in Kashmir to stay. It will always affect some elements of Kashmir's society one way or the other. *The best confidence building measure will be to offer progressive and constructive ideas.*

The policy challenge is complex. We cannot leave everything to the government. Civil society has a crucial responsibility to help Kashmiri youth understand the right path in life. We must support those voices rising from Kashmir which make impassioned pleas for a shared inclusive society. Evil triumphs when good men do nothing.

A Third Party

It is known that India will not agree to third-party intervention in Kashmir. For decades, India has been consistent in its policy that Kashmir is a bilateral issue between India and Pakistan, and has to be resolved through bilateral talks. Pakistan is always vouching for third party intervention despite committing itself to peaceful resolution of all issues bilaterally, through the Shimla Agreement and other declarations.

Kashmiri separatists and their underground and overground forces toe the Pakistan line. This has created a unique narrative in Kashmir – *the localisation of foreign affairs.* Kashmiris across the political divide keep talking about the perceived threat to international peace posed by the Kashmir conflict. They talk of the South-Asian region, the international community, UN Resolution on Kashmir and so forth.

A political worker who has not even been introduced to his mohalla or village talks about the larger south Asian region. *This psyche has built misplaced narratives in Kashmir.* India must be blamed squarely for this. *The Government of India has not been able to present its case before the Kashmiris in a holistic way with constitutional and legal documentation.* The government has contended itself with issuing statements that have offended Kashmiri society and alienated it further. The *atoot ang* politics has been honoured more in breach than its observance. This has shattered the confidence of Kashmiris to levels beyond imagination.

The institutions of dialogue have become suspect. That is why Kashmiris do not show any interest now in engagement through dialogue.

The main objective should be to build trust, understand the real interests of the Kashmiris, and help them understand their aims better. This can help in overcoming most of the concerns that make parties reluctant to come to the negotiating table.

In a place like Kashmir where Pakistan too is a stakeholder, there are a number of groups and forces that have the potential to frustrate the government's ability to open contact with militant groups. In Kashmir, you cannot achieve any breakthrough by talking to over-ground separatists. They are only an extension of Pakistan and represent Pakistan's interests in Kashmir.

Suggesting Indo-Pak dialogue is not my domain. I suggest direct contact with the militants. They can help in changing the situation in Kashmir for the better.

Who will talk to them? I don't undermine the ability of Indian negotiators. The problem is about perception. Militants will not agree to talk to Indian negotiators publicly. If you are not doing anything publicly in Kashmir, you will fail. Even about the participation in elections to prove the 'representative character', Kashmir separatists demand supervision by international players.

The Indian government's stated position is that 'talks and terror cannot go together'. Kashmiri separatists say 'no talks till India accepts the disputed nature' of Kashmir. The problem is on two fronts. The question is how to move forward without compromising on the basic premises?

In a turnaround, which perhaps most will not expect, the Indian government should engage the services of a foreign negotiator. This 'foreigner' or 'third party' should be someone with proven ability to talk to militants. S/he should be able to talk to militants on both sides of the Line of Control in Kashmir on the behalf of the Government of India. It is not the government which shall do the talking. Similarly, militants will talk to the foreign negotiator. They won't be talking to the Indian government. *Both sides will be communicating with each other*, but not talking to each other.

This can help in building legitimate contacts in the long run. AS Dulat says in his book that *double agents are the best assets if you don't have direct contacts*. In Kashmir's case, only a Kashmiri can be a double agent. But a Kashmiri double agent will not be able to build confidence on either side because of the inherent perceptional challenges. So the need for a 'foreigner'.

The homogeneity of Kashmir society has contributed in building narrow, irrational and mythical narratives.

How to attempt reversing this tide? It is unfortunate that the Indian civil society, the most important stakeholder in Kashmir, has not realised its responsibility in this regard. There are several groups in the mainland who have played an active role in Kashmir. But when they reach out to Kashmir individually, their efforts are unable to impact the situation. There should be collegiums of these groups to reach out to the younger generation in Kashmir in an impactful manner. These groups should mobilise people in the mainland to reach out to the Kashmiri youth. They should help the Kashmiri youth to analyse and understand what they need. More and more civil society groups can be aligned with development projects in Kashmir. Journalists, authors, former bureaucrats and other eminent civil society members should be encouraged to talk to Kashmiri youth in large numbers. Colleges, universities and schools should be the main focus of the Indian civil society members. Such interactions will help in removing obstacles for future engagement.

Reurn of the Pandits to Kashmir

Second, the issue of the return of Kashmiri Pandits should be linked to restoration of the plural character of Kashmiri society. This is a humanitarian issue. Their coming back can become a matter of strength if there is sincerity of purpose. Large groups of Kashmiri Pandits should be encouraged to visit their ancestral places frequently.

This way, direct interactions will take place between the two communities, which will remove mistrust. There can also be cultural programmes where the participation of Kashmiri Pandits can be facilitated in large numbers. Close interactions between estranged neighbours will lead to better understanding.

The Kashmiri Pandits living in migrant camps in Jammu should be part of such programmes, and not the elites in their community. These initiatives can help in building an atmosphere conducive for the future engagements. As I have mentioned in detail elsewhere in the book, Kashmir, with the exodus of Kashmiri Pandits, is a homogenous society today. There are only Muslims and Muslims around. The homogeneity actually blocks the mental space for accepting the beauty of diversity, particularly in Muslim majority societies. Unless there is a demographic shift, Kashmir's centuries old heterogeneity cannot return.

Retuning Sufis to Kashmir

The Jammu and Kashmir government should introduce the teachings of Nooruddin Reshi and Lal Ded in the school and college curriculum in consultation with educationists. The teachings of these icons of Kashmir's plural cultural ethos can help in restoring the social order.

Returning Education to Schools, Colleges

Reputed universities across the country should be involved in designing exchange programmes with educational institutions in Kashmir. *There is a desperate need for improving the level of education in this region.*

Kashmir needs an intermingling of ideas. How to improve the standard of education with better teaching of mathematics, science and humanities? How to provide better opportunities for jobs and employment? This will minimises the chances of youth falling into the trap of radical extremism.

The ability to think critically is needed crucially in Kashmir.

This will enable the youth to see through the drawbacks and flaws in the logic of uneducated but charismatic radical preachers and imams. This is also important in the context of the ideology of 'us versus them'. The indoctrination by Jamaat-e-Islami and other Salafist groups in Kashmir has constructed social narratives based on hatred for others.

We need to ensure more and more interactions between the students of mainland India and Kashmiri students at university and college levels. Toxic social narratives can be countered with those based on strong scientific reasoning. *There is also the need to ensure that the Maududi interpretation or the Wahabi worldview is not legitimised in colleges and universities.*

The education system in Kashmir needs overhauling. It must be much broader so that the right education can be imparted to students. There are sustained efforts in Kashmir to transfer the bloody conflict to the coming generations. There is need to rise to the occasion and offer solutions based on education. I have been maintaining since long that women achievers from the mainland could play an important role in de-radicalisation of women in Kashmir. Cultural, literary, educational interactions are very important to broaden the worldview of Kashmir women.

Outsource Sadbhavna Programme to Civil Society

The Army's *Sadhbavna* programme should be outsourced to Indian civil society groups excluding Kashmiris.

This is important for both social and political reasons. Whatever good is done by the Army is perceived as a conspiracy. If the same projects are outsourced to honest and reputed civil society groups of the mainland, it will have a larger, more positive impact. This will also help in developing proximity between the local population and Indian citizenry.

The Ministry of Tourism should start a goodwill tourism programme for Kashmir, where it can send ambassadors of all States to Kashmir and encourage their regular interactions with people associated and dependent on the tourism industry in Kashmir.

Involve Jamaat-e-Islami Hind in Kashmir

Jamaat-e-Islami Hind should be involved in rationalising the narratives in Kashmir. This is urgently required to restore social order here.

Jamaat-e-Islami-Hind is familiar with the art of living peacefully in a pluralist society. It is easier for political extremes to make efforts for lasting peace, rather than moderates. This is because no one can challenge the political extremes for the compromises they make.

Jamaat-e-Islami is the fountainhead of extremism in Kashmir. Jamaat-e-Islami Hind knows how to coexist in a plural India. It can prevail in redefining political theology in Kashmir.

Jamaat-e-Islami is the most vibrant theological forum in Kashmir. Some may find my suggestion of outreach towards the Jamaat contradictory. We also know that Jamaat used the truce agreement of 2000 between them and the Indian deep state to the best of their advantage.

I am not suggesting any pact here.

Our objective is to see whether Jamaat-e-Islami Hind can help in mainstreaming its Kashmir chapter for acceptance of an inclusive, pluralist India.

There should be periodic, planned shifts and exchange programmes between the faculties of Jammu University and Kashmir University. It is essential to narrow the regional divide through intellectual discourse, understand the contending narratives and evolve a common rational narrative. Also with organisations like Jamia Milia.

There is a mushrooming of orphanages across Kashmir Valley. There seem to be more orphanages in Kashmir than orphans. These orphanages are actually money-minting centers where innocent orphans are radicalised and deeply Islamised. Government of India's Ministry of Social Justice and Empowerment and its HRD Ministry should perhaps monitor these as it does for orphanages in all of the other 29 States and 7 Union Territories of India and be more greatly involved in women and children's education in Kashmir as it does in rest of India.

The government should provide hostel facilities for all orphans, provide them free education in government schools and *close the orphanages*. With the right education, these orphans can be raised as good global citizens.

The Media

The media is playing an important role in shaping narratives the world over. Kashmir is no exception. The problem is that anchors on some leading national television channels endorse the Hindutva worldview as much as the Kashmir media endorses the extremist Muslim sentiment. Both are validating violent ideologies.

The Kashmir media's position against these offensive news channels is 'God versus evil'. The *godi* media, on the other hand, pitches its Kashmir coverage as 'good versus evil'. This has dangerous consequences for the overall situation in Kashmir. *The national media and the Kashmir media – both are playing to the gallery and giving their respective audiences what they want. Both have failed to understand their responsibilities in terms of adhering to the long-term good of the society.* It is like the outbreak of an epidemic, where doctors are prescribing ways in which the epidemic may spread further.

The media must be aware of the consequences of its actions. Since 2016, the romanticisation of *jihadi*s by the local media and the glorification of army men caught in the line of fire by the national media have led to xenophobia of specific target groups. The deadly but misplaced narratives of romanticisation of militancy by Kashmir media and glorification of the military men getting killed in the line of duty by the national TV channels has damaged the situation in Kashmir beyond redemption. The mullahs in Kashmir have complete control over the Kashmir press, so has the Sangh Parivar on Prime time.

Now it is very apparent that the jingoistic media here and there are as detrimental to the peace as the deadly narrative of Islamisation of Kashmir and Hinduisation of India. The peace-loving constituency shrinks day by day. In such a radicalised atmosphere, peaceniks can only hope that the media realises how toxic jingoism is for overall peace in the region.

For Kashmir to be a part of peaceful India, a carefully

crafted sociologically pro-active and scientifically viable peace plan is urgently needed, if necessary, a global intervention (like the Irish American intervention in northern Ireland or EU in Yugoslavia).Women, children and the media are the 'target population' for creating a future for Kashmir and I can only pray that the world is listening.

About the Author

A brilliant student, the favourite of his teachers in the village high school, **Bashir Assad** fell to the extremist Jamaat-e-Islami ideology soon after passing Class X with distinction. The boy who had charmed his entire hamlet with his keen intellect was seen giving sermons in mosques, preaching Maududi Islam.

His clan, the village folk – all had great expectations from him. Some hoped he would join the administrative services. Others wanted him to take up medicine and be a doctor. Many others saw a future political leader in the making, on account of his impressive oratory skills. Some would even tease him to go to Bollywood, given his Kashmiri good looks and charm.

Influenced by the Jamaat leaders of Anantnag district, at the age of 17 Bashir was a completely changed young man. Deeply indoctrinated, his sole objective was living a pious Islamic life, and continue giving sermons in mosques.

In 1989, Kashmir valley slipped into the hands of armed militia. This jolted Bashir out of the religious stupor. He saw indoctrinated young men of south Kashmir march into militancy with bravado, taking up a life of ghastly violence. As they were killed, more followed them. Bashir was shaken.

He realised how dangerous the Jamaat ideology was for the blossoming youth of Kashmir. He disassociated with the Jamaat and raised his voice against the newly-imported culture of Kalashnikovs.

Bashir had lived the ideology of Maududi Islam for about three years. When he came out of the daze of indoctrination, he realised that he had lost several very valuable years of his young life. He was aware that while he was able to escape the grip of extreme religious thought, thousands of youth of his generation had not been so fortunate. They had thrown away their youth and shattered the happy dreams of their parents by choosing the gun. This searing pain never left Bashir.

Drawn to journalism, Bashir studied Mass Communication in New Delhi. Back home, he joined a local vernacular newspaper and also started making documentaries for Doordarshan.

Bashir started writing and speaking out against the killings perpetrated by both security forces and militants. He became a journalist, activist and motivational orator.

He had experienced the consequences of indoctrination at an early age. Through his writings, workshops, conferences and seminars, Bashir constantly reached out to the youth. Presenting himself as a test case, he would caution the youth not to fall prey to this deadly ideology.

For his writings against the excesses of militants and also the security forces, Bashir was targeted by both. He was falsely implicated by the Special Operations Group of Jammu and Kashmir Police and was given third degree torture for 35 days in an investigation cell.

Targeted by militants, Bashir survived five attempts on his life. He was kidnapped four times by militants at the behest of local Jamaatis. Twice, he escaped from the custody of militants.

On one occasion, Bashir escaped with the help of a woman from a village who covered him with her hijab and provided him an escape route.

These attempts on his life did not deter Bashir from his chosen path. He continued to work to strengthen the ideology of reconciliation and not confrontation for addressing the problems Kashmir faced socially and politically.

Bashir worked closely with late J&K chief minister Mufti Sayeed for a couple of years. He left active politics disillusioned, realising that political leaders in Kashmir were doing politics on human blood. In 2011, Bashir launched a platform for the youth under the banner of Lehar (an NGO).

Since then, he has been involved in interactions between members of the Indian civil society and students in Kashmir. His objective has been to rationalise the political ambitions of Kashmiri youth, and give them platforms to channelise their energy in a constructive manner.